Foster's
WELSH
ODDITIES

Foster's
WELSH
ODDITIES

ALLEN FOSTER

ROBERT HALE • LONDON

© Allen Foster 2015
First published in Great Britain 2015

ISBN 978-0-7198-1754-0

Robert Hale Limited
Clerkenwell House
Clerkenwell Green
London EC1R 0HT

www.halebooks.com

All illustrations © Doug Ferris 2015

A catalogue record for this book is available from the British Library

2 4 6 8 10 9 7 5 3 1

Printed and bound by
CPI Antony Rowe, Chippenham and Eastbourne

To Jonathan Williams

Acknowledgements

FOSTER'S WELSH ODDITIES is a collection of strange Welsh trivia. It's a bit like a Welsh version of the wonderful *Ripley's Believe It or Not!* books that were once extremely popular. Robert Ripley had an amazing time travelling the world looking for strange facts. I made do with looking though old books, newspapers and archives in various libraries and online. If you like this book, you will love the *Fortean Times* (www.forteantimes.com), a monthly magazine dedicated to the weird and unusual.

Painstaking efforts have been made to ensure that all the bizarre trivia within *Foster's Welsh Oddities* is correct. In a book with so many facts, it would be hard to believe that some errors have not been made. If you spot any mistakes or would like to contribute any strange facts, please send them to the author, c/o Robert Hale publishers.

Jonathan Williams, Doug Ferris, Michael Potterton, Sophie Hayley, everyone at Robert Hale and many other unsung heroes deserve credit for their part in this book's creation.

PATRICK NEARY FROM Aberdare, Glamorgan, had his right ear bitten off in a fight in Dover on 4 October 1991. The 32-year-old's ear was so badly damaged that surgeons at the Queen Victoria Hospital in East Grinstead did not think any operation to reattach it immediately would be successful, so they temporarily stitched the cartilage of the ear inside Neary's right thigh to maintain its blood supply. Neary was working as an electrician on the Channel Tunnel at the time of the fight. He was due to have the ear reattached to its rightful place in February 1992, but the hospital could not get in contact with him, so they had to use the media to track him down.

IMAGINE THEIR SURPRISE when burglars broke into a cottage at Ewenny near Bridgend, Glamorgan, in July 1988 and found nothing inside. It was merely a mocked-up façade supported by scaffolding and was being used by Harlech Television during the filming of a drama.

A COW CLIMBED some sixty feet up a spiral staircase to the top of the control tower at Swansea Flying Club on 26 July 1956 and remained there for sixteen hours. While it gazed contentedly over the countryside, authorities below wondered how to get the cow down. 'We had a cow up there before,' a member of the flying club said. 'That time I helped to push her down the stairway. But this time we are not going to risk that because there is a danger of being crushed against the wall if the cow gets angry.'

John Davis, a 17-year-old farm boy, managed to solve the problem. He milked the cow, then coaxed her down the stairs by making encouraging 'moo' sounds.

IN AUGUST 1989 a Swansea judge awarded damages of £1,000 to a 74-year-old woman who claimed that her champion white poodle produced black puppies because a breeder switched stud dogs during mating. Mrs Helen Worth had paid dog breeder Peter Parkinson £100 to have her pedigree white poodle Caro mated with his pedigree white poodle Geoffrey. When the two dogs were introduced, neither party showed any interest. While Mrs Worth waited outside, Parkinson took the two dogs into a clipping room. Thirty minutes later he returned with Caro, claiming that the two dogs had mated. Nine weeks later Caro gave birth to six healthy *black* puppies.

Black pups were worth less than a sixth of the money purebred pedigree white ones would bring, so Mrs Worth sued for damages. In his defence, Parkinson claimed that the two white dogs had mated, adding that it was possible for two white poodles to produce black puppies. 'In the litters I have bred, I have always had mixed colours. I have had colours of the rainbow', he said. Parkinson also suggested that Caro may not have been true to her pedigree – a statement Judge Gibbon thought highly unlikely given that the dog was kept behind two 6-foot fences.

A geneticist brought in as an expert witness said that the chances of two white dogs producing black puppies were about 10 million to one, concluding that it was most likely a black poodle had sired the litter. When the case began, one of Caro's black puppies, Ricky, was brought into the court at the request of Judge Gibbon, a former dog breeder himself. Ricky offered a paw and the judge shook it.

On 16 October 2009, *The Sun* revealed that an image of magician and comedy genius Tommy Cooper (1921–84) appeared on the bottom of a steak pie in his hometown of Caerphilly, Glamorgan.

A group of women and children staged an ingenious robbery in August 1977. They walked into a jewellery shop in Rhyl, Flintshire, opened a cardboard box and out flew a pigeon. While the shop's two sales assistants tried to catch the bird, the women furtively picked up rings worth £600, caught the pigeon and walked out.

In 1897, the Dock and Harbour Master of Newport, Monmouthshire, married a Miss Hunter from the town. They spent their honeymoon at Dawlish in Devon, where she lost her gold bracelet while swimming in the sea. The couple revisited the beach in 1925 and, while sitting in deckchairs, spotted a glint of gold in the sand as the tide went out. It was the lost bracelet!

Fifteen years after appearing in the same photograph as strangers, Debbie Baker and her close friend Linda Lloyd discovered the coincidence after browsing through photographs taken on a 1990 holiday in Spain. Linda was in the background of several pictures. At the time they were taken, the women happened to be drinking in the same bar. Debbie and four friends from Bournemouth were in Benalmadena on the Costa del Sol, while Linda, from Manchester, was on honeymoon there with her husband Alan. Debbie moved to Denbigh in 1993 and Linda arrived in the town nine years later. They became friends when working as classroom assistants in the same school, but neither realized that their paths had crossed before.

IVOR CARTER FROM Newport, Monmouthshire, was examining a revolver in December 1920 when the weapon suddenly went off, firing a bullet into his chest. The 21-year-old began to cough violently. A few minutes later Carter coughed up the bullet. He later made a full recovery.

WHAT IS IT with Wrexham postmen and post boxes? Ceris Jones was walking past a post box in Wrexham in September 1971 when she heard frantic hammering. She looked around but could not see anyone. 'Then I realized the knocking was coming from inside the post box', Ceris said. 'I could hardly believe it, but I knew someone was trapped inside.' She knelt beside the box and called 'Hello'. No one replied, but the knocking got louder. Ceris ran to a nearby post office and sought help. At first she was not believed, but she managed to convince an inspector to investigate. Minutes later the combined post box and stamp machine was opened and an embarrassed postman was freed. He told his rescuers that he had been filling the stamp machine when the wind blew the door shut. He had been trapped only for a short while.

Another postman was trapped inside a large postbox in Wrexham in October 1998 for nearly half an hour after a gust of wind blew the door shut. He was discovered when 72-year-old pensioner Alf France went to post a letter into the box and a hand came out to take it and a voice inside cried out for help. France found the keys still outside and released the postman.

ON 5 DECEMBER 1664, a boat crossing the Menai Strait between Anglesey and Caernarvonshire was sunk, with 81 passengers on board. Only one escaped, and his name was Hugh Williams. On 5 December 1785 another boat was sunk under the same circumstances. It had 60 passengers on board, and all were lost except one person. His name Hugh Williams. On 5 August 1820 another ship sank with 25 passengers on board. There was only one survivor; astonishingly his name too was Hugh Williams.

THE ROUND HOUSE near the harbour in Barmouth, Merionethshire, is a curious relic of a bygone age. It was built as a lock-up in 1834 and was last used in 1861. The circular stone prison had two cells – one for men and one for women – and was mainly used to hold drunks or offenders as they were waiting to be moved to the local courts or county jail at Dolgellau. With thick stone walls and only two slits for windows, it must have made for an excellent prison.

THE LANDLORD OF a pub in Towcester, Somerset, Mr Dowlen (originally from Merionethshire) became famous for a wager he won on 8 November 1808. For the princely sum of one hundred guineas, Dowlen bet he could walk

500 miles in seven days on ground of his own choosing. The wager was accepted and the Welsh publican set off on 1 November. He completed the walk in the allotted time and won his wager having covered the distance through Berkshire, Wiltshire, Somerset, Devon and Dorset, finishing up in Hampshire. The tough Welsh pedestrian was described as being 'stoutly made' and only 5 feet tall.

AFTER PICKING UP a load of iron ore at Wabama in Newfoundland, the steamer *Saxilby* set out for Port Talbot in Glamorgan, but she was fated never to reach her destination. Some 400 miles west of Ireland, the *Saxilby* was lost at sea with all hands during a severe storm on 15 November 1933.

More than two years later, the last message of a seaman on board the tragic ship washed up on Aberaeron beach, Cardiganshire within a mile of his home. The seaman's name was Joe Okane and he was one of the crew of twenty-nine aboard the *Saxilby*. The message was found inside a cocoa tin by fishermen out digging for bait. It was addressed to Okane's family and read: '*S.S. Saxilby* sinking off Irish coast. Love to sisters, brothers, and Dinah. Joe Okane.'

ON 12 MARCH 1978 the Dublin Welsh Male Voice Choir managed to come second in a choral contest – despite being the only entrants. The choir had entered in two sections of a competition that took place in Arklow, Co. Wicklow. They planned to sing Richard Wagner's 'Roman War Song' in the open section and a medley of Welsh hymns in the sacred music section. As events later showed, even the best-laid plans do not always work out as intended.

On arrival in the town, the choir went to the Arklow Bay Hotel, where they had allegedly reserved rehearsal facilities. Finding another choir using their room, the Dublin Welsh males adjourned to the bar until the room became available.

Later, a stern-faced contest organizer burst into the rehearsal room as the choir was running through a few pieces and angrily told them they were late for the competition. They raced up, bounded onto the stage and prepared to give the performance of their lives. Unfortunately, their conductor did not know which competition section this was and never bothered to ask. Under his able direction, the choir launched into a rendition of Wagner's 'Roman War Song'. Only after they had finished did they realize that they had been singing in the sacred music section! The adjudicator was forgiving and made favourable remarks on what was a well-sung, though highly inappropriate, piece. The choir had been the only entry in this section, and it seemed to all they would (naturally) win it.

The authorities displayed great unease at the prospect at awarding first prize to the Dublin Welsh. Instead, they awarded them *second* prize, which was a cheque for £40 and no cup. (First prize had been a cup and £80.) During the week, one of the choir related the bizarre story to a journalist friend. The journalist rang the contest organizers in Arklow to confirm that the only entry in a competition had come second. 'What are they complaining about?' the organizers asked. It later featured in the *Daily Mirror*, which gave the choir £50 for the story. Since second prize had been £40, with the addition of the *Daily Mirror* money the Dublin Welsh Male Voice Choir managed to come out ahead, despite being second in what was a one-horse race.

LLANBADARN MAGISTRATE CAPTAIN C.F. Harrington Churchill told reporters in July 1963, 'My conscience is perfectly clear' after acquitting Roy Langford of careless driving, allegedly committed while he was driving home from a party at the magistrate's home.

IN 1765 NEWSPAPERS reported the death of a remarkable Glamorgan woman who had died aged 128 years. Mary John from Llantwit Major was said to have milked cows up until six years before her death.

ALBERT GRABHAM'S FORGETFULNESS cost him dearly on New Year's Day 1989. He was working as a chef at the New House Hotel in Haverfordwest, Pembrokeshire. He hid the New Year's Eve takings of £200 inside an oven for safety, and then forgot about them. The next morning, when Grabham turned on the oven to prepare lunch, he incinerated the money.

THE GRAVEYARD OF Strata Florida, a Cistercian abbey in Cardiganshire, contains two curious graves. The first contains the leg of a local man and the inscription on its headstone reads: 'The left leg and part of the thigh of Henry Hughes, cooper, cut off and interr'd here June 18th 1756.' Hughes lost his leg in a farming accident and later emigrated to America – where the rest of him is buried.

The story concerning the second grave is more poignant.

In 1929 the frozen body of an unknown soldier who had served in the Afghan wars in the 1880s was found in the hills north of the abbey. All the unidentified man had in his pocket was a photograph of a young girl and a copy of *Old Moore's Almanack*. The unfortunate stranger was buried in the graveyard by the local people and a headstone with the following beautiful epitaph was erected:

> He died upon the hillside drear
> Alone, where snow was deep.
> By strangers he was carried here
> Where princes also sleep.

In JULY 1974 coastguards stationed at Rhyl, Flintshire, dispatched a boat when they saw a distress signal flying aloft on a yacht out to sea. When they reached the vessel, they were met by an embarrassed yachtsman in his underpants, who explained that he did not know that his wet trousers, hoisted aloft to dry in the wind, formed an official rescue signal.

IN A VINDICTIVE, yet curiously generous will, Richard Crawshay of Cyfartha, Glamorgan, who died in 1810, 'cut off' his only son with £100,000, on the grounds that he had 'spurned his counsel, withheld his confidence, and insolently entreated him on many occasions. In consideration of all of which he had determined he should be neither his executor nor residuary legatee, as he had heretofore intended and written.'

A REMARKABLE WEDDING took place at St Martin-in-the-Fields in London in 1719. The bridegroom was forty-one years old, and 25 inches tall, Robert Skinner from Ripon in Yorkshire. His Welsh bride, Judith, was just an inch taller. The Skinners had been happily married for twenty-three years and had a family of fourteen children when they came to public prominence, exhibiting themselves in London. The curious flocked to see them and the couple earned a great deal of money. After two years they had accumulated enough to retire comfortably. They travelled around in a small carriage, drawn by two dogs and driven by a small boy in yellow and purple livery.

After Judith died in 1763, Robert was grief-stricken. He shut himself up in a room for over a year, refusing to see anyone except a faithful old retainer who looked after him. When he emerged from his seclusion, Robert left London and went back to Yorkshire, where he died two years later, leaving a fortune of £22,000 to be equally divided among his children.

WEST FLINT LOCAL officials apologized to local Conservative MP Nigel Birch in November 1968 for accidentally locking him out of a charity ball, of which he was the guest of honour. Birch arrived late with his wife. When he knocked, then banged on the entrance door, there was no response, so they drove home. An official was quoted as saying, 'It was most unfortunate.'

A TREE SAVED the life of a boy at Llandudno, Caernarvonshire, on 11 September 1928. The boy was climbing on rocks near the summit of the Great Orme, a promontory to the west of the town, when he slipped and fell down a cliff. Luckily he landed in the branches of a tree some sixty feet below and was merely scratched.

THE OCCUPANTS OF a house in Carmarthen had an unexpected visitor in the shape of a bullock. The animal was one of a number of cattle being driven through the town around 5 o'clock on the morning of 14 November 1817. It broke away from the drovers and fell from a height near Castlegreen onto the roof of a house where the occupants were asleep. As might be expected, the family's terror was great when part of the roof caved in. However, luck was on their side.

Although the roof fell, the bullock remained aloft, held there by a thick beam directly above a bed in which two children were fast asleep. While the bullock balanced precariously overhead, the parents rescued their children. The children had hardly been moved to safety when the beam broke and bullock and all fell onto the bed where the children had been. Thankfully no one was injured and the bullock was only a little dazed by its misadventure.

TREVOR GEORGE FROM Penarth, Glamorgan, was evidently a keen soccer fan. In December 1982 he named his newborn daughter after twenty of the world's greatest soccer players – to his wife's despair. In tears she went home to her mother. 'I never expected him to give a girl those sort of names', said Lynette George. Her husband had registered his daughter's names as: 'Jennifer Edson Arantes do Nascimento (Pelé)

Jairzinho Rivelino Carlos-Alberto Paulo-César Brietner Cruyff Greaves Charlton Best Moore Ball Keegan Banks Gray Francis Brooking Curtis Toshack Law George'.

Mrs George managed to cancel the registration and give her daughter the more sensible name of Jennifer Anne George. 'I'm more angry about her changing the names than about her leaving', her husband said. 'She can stay where she is if that's what she's going to do.'

AFRAID OF BEING sent back to prison on firearms charges, ex-convict Lawrence Steer from Cardiff jumped bail in 1965 and went into hiding – unaware that he need not have bothered evading the law. A blanket pardon for such offences was in effect and he would have been released from detention. In 1972 Steer, 'visibly aged by worry', gave himself up. A judge gave him a two-month suspended jail term and Steer had to pay the £50 he had forfeited when he failed to appear in court three years earlier.

IN FEBRUARY 1921, Mrs Jenkins, the wife of a stonemason from Fleur-de-lis in Monmouthshire, regained her sight after being blind for twenty-two years. She had been struck by lightning in 1898 and mysteriously lost her sight a year later. Mrs Jenkins occasionally went into trances, some of which lasted for as long as fourteen days. Doctors believed her recovery would be permanent.

WHEN CARDIFF-BORN WRITER Ken Follett was researching his epic novel *The Pillars of the Earth* he came across a fascinating book by the French writer Jean Gimpel called *The Cathedral Builders*. Follett wrote to Gimpel to hire him as a historical consultant and was astonished to discover that they lived on the same street in London.

ON 1 MARCH 1913 the Welsh military authorities were the victim of a hoax. They received apparently authentic instructions from high command to begin the mobilization of all soldiers in Wales and place them on a war footing. The order was promptly relayed to all troops stationed across the country, and arrangements for billeting in centralized locations were well underway before the hoax was discovered.

IN JULY 1765 a cow belonging to William Vaughn of Bettws Abergele in Denbighshire gave birth to a two-headed calf. The animal's body was normal, but it had two necks and two heads, four eyes, four ears and two mouths. For several days the calf thrived, but then it died. The heads drank at different times.

BRECON TOWN COUNCIL ordered a petrol station to remove its 'talking' self-service fuel pumps in June 1972 because they kept neighbours awake. Whenever a motorist pulled in at night, a tape recording would tell them how to operate the self-service system. Neighbours were still not satisfied at the authority's intervention as they still were awoken by noisy motorists slamming doors.

On 23 October 1848 a miner at the Pentrefelen pit near Llangyfelach, Glamorgan, almost killed himself and several other co-workers because of his own stupidity. On that day the miner brought food for his lunch and a pot of strong tea. In a similar pot he carried 1½ lb of gunpowder to be used for blasting purposes. At lunchtime the miner absent-mindedly put the wrong teapot over the fire and the results can be imagined. It exploded and badly burnt the miner and five other men. Fortunately, none of the injuries were life-threatening.

In September 1966 Harry Diaper from Newport placed an advertisement in his local paper informing readers that he was very much alive. 'There's been a rumour going around that I'm dead', he said. 'People have been looking at me as if they had seen a ghost.'

Farmer Gordon Griffiths from Clydach, Glamorgan, moved a live unexploded World War II bomb off his land on 6 December 1988 because he did not want bomb-disposal experts trampling his newly sown field of grass.

'I know it was a silly thing to do, but it was just on the spur of the moment', he explained two days after the bomb experts defused the device and found its detonator intact.

Griffiths said he had accidentally struck the bomb with a pickaxe while working on his farm. He called the police, but then decided to move the bomb himself to the edge of the field. Griffiths told reporters that he was 'sweating and frightened' as he carried the 30-inch bomb over 200 feet to the edge of the field, but took a chance that he was safe enough to do so as the pickaxe had not already detonated it. 'I knew what these police and bomb-disposal people would be like, and I was worried about my grass. I'm just a down-to-earth farmer and I wanted to keep my land tidy.'

A police spokesman said they did not recommend anyone do what the farmer had done, for obvious reasons.

STEVE BRIERS FROM the village of Kilgetty in Pembrokeshire set a bizarre world record on 6 February 1990 by reciting the entire lyrics of Queen's album *A Night at the Opera* backwards on BBC North West Radio 4 'Cat's Whiskers', in a time of 9 minutes and 58 seconds.

RETURNING HOME AFTER work at an Ebbw Vale colliery on February 1924, a miner saw a sight that stopped him dead in his tracks. He spotted two rats, each holding one end of a piece of straw. The miner threw a piece of wood he was carrying, killing one rat, but the other one did not move. Intrigued, the man investigated and realized the remaining rat had no eyes and was being led along by the other rat.

IN JANUARY 1973 10-year-old Paul Butler from Wrexham was carrying home a goldfish in a plastic bag when the bus conductor asked him for one penny extra 'for the pet'. Paul's mother was furious at the bus conductor's pettiness. 'It is ridiculous to have to pay a bus fare for a fish', she said. A bus company spokesman said that 'pets must be paid for, but goldfish do not come into this category'.

MABEL SLOCOMBE OF Fern Street, Ogmore Vale, Glamorgan, was crippled at birth and remained that way until the age of thirty-nine, when she was cured in an unexpected manner. In December 1949 Mabel wrenched her back while turning a mangle. A few hours later she stopped limping and began walking normally for the first time in her life. Previously one leg had been longer than the other and one arm had been 2 inches longer than the other.

THE *STRAND MAGAZINE* for February 1903 contains a letter from the Reverend David Lloyd of Llangollen, Denbighshire, who wrote about a remarkable coincidence in his family. His three children were born on the same date in different years. Myfanwy was born on 21 January 1900, Nesta on 21 January 1901, and Robert on 21 January 1902. Not only that – they were all born at 2 a.m.

IN THE SPACE of three days in August 2007, Ray Mackenzie, his wife Gill and 14-year-old son Sam all scored holes-in-one at Llanfairfechan Golf Club near their home in Caernarvonshire. The odds of such an occurrence are said to be 15 million to one. In 2006 Dafydd Owen scored two holes-in-one in one round at the same golf club.

MEDICAL LITERATURE CONTAINS numerous, but unverified, cases of septuagenarian mothers. One such case is that of 72-year-old Ellen Ellis of Four Crosses, Denbighshire, who allegedly gave birth to a child on 15 May 1776 in her forty-sixth year of marriage. She already had twelve children by the same father, the oldest being forty-five and the youngest twenty-five. The report says the thirteenth child was stillborn owing to the mother being frightened by a man a fortnight earlier, who had told her that, if she was with child, it was by the devil. Mrs Ellis and her husband were described as being very infirm. It has been suggested that many late births were really illegitimate grandchildren.

THE NEIGHBOURS OF a factory at Aberaman, Glamorgan, which made smokeless fuel demanded that the National Coal Board close it in June 1965 – because the smoke spewing from the factory was blackening everything in the surrounding area.

A DARNING NEEDLE and thread emerged from the ankle of a young Abergavenny woman sixteen years after it had entered her arm, *The Times* of 20 February 1843 reported. During all that time she had never suffered any discomfort, but since its removal her leg was very painful and inflamed. The needle was reportedly much smaller than when it went in and was very bent.

ON 5 AUGUST 1974 the Dolgellau darts league in Merionethshire banned women's teams because they might create a baby-sitting problem for the men's teams. 'If the wives get into the league, who is to stop at home to look after the children?' asked league president Arthur Dunn.

FOR MORE THAN a year a husband and wife lived in a wooden kennel at Ystrad Mynach, Glamorgan. It measured 7 × 5 feet and was one of four in the corner of a disused allotment. The other three were occupied by the couple's dogs. On 5 June 1953 Caerphilly Council gave the couple a week to leave the kennel. Dr W.R. Nash, the medical officer, said: 'The position is incompatible with any standard of housing.' The couple moved into the kennel after vacating two rooms in a neighbouring village and had been unable to find another home where they could continue breeding their prize-winning dogs.

HEADING HOME FROM Monmouth late at night on 28 October 1848, after drinking with a friend, a man called Freeman tried to avoid paying a toll at a bridge by crossing a river. However, the river was swollen from recent heavy rains and, in his drunken condition, Freeman was not able to cross it and fell in. He was saved by a fortunate circumstance. Poachers fishing downriver heard the splash as the drunken man fell in and assumed that it was a salmon stirring. They immediately spread and threw out their net and caught what they believed to be a salmon. After considerable effort, they hauled in the net and discovered to their surprise that they had caught a drunken man. Freeman was alive and the poachers carried him to Monmouth where he recovered, a little wiser than before.

A LEGAL ACTION was laughed out of a Swansea court by a judge on 11 December 1963. David Thomas sold David Roberts a derelict railway station which he did not own and Roberts paid for it with a worthless cheque. The judge called it a draw and sent the men on their way. In evidence, Thomas told the judge that he believed he owned the abandoned railway station because he had paid another man £14 for it. He sold it to Roberts for £84. Roberts paid for it by cheque and had the railway station half-torn down for his scrap-iron business when a policeman came along and stopped work after Roberts' cheque had bounced.

JOHN LOWNDES FROM Pembrokeshire used to love his daily pot of tea with Ian, his father. In 2008, ten years after his father's death, John was once again able to have a pot of tea with his father after he had Ian's ashes made into a teapot. John had been unable to decide on a fitting resting place for his father's ashes. Then he was introduced to potter Neil Richardson, whose firm, Here in Spirit, made ceramic urns and vases using the ashes of the deceased. Richardson mixed his father's ashes straight into the clay so that the teapot was safe to drink from.

On 31 July 1988 the Royal Air Force rescued twenty-two stranded bird-watchers from Bardsey Island, two miles off the Caernarvonshire coast, a week after they had been stranded there by bad weather. Two RAF helicopters picked up the group and took them to Pwllheli.

In 1746 Reeves Williams from Cardigan called himself the 'Man Ostrich' and performed feats of swallowing for select audiences, who paid him sixpence a head to view him swallowing stones, pieces of iron, nails and many other objects. Williams was described as a 27-year-old labouring man – 'a stout hale fellow, of very ruddy complexion'. His main trick was to swallow and regurgitate four pieces of iron he had specially made. They were 1¼ inches long and ¾ inch wide and were very thick. After exhibiting himself across Wales, Williams was last recorded in November 1746 as heading for London to try his luck there.

On 27 January 1988 a coal miner freed a 2-year-old terrier named Rocky which had been trapped for eight days about forty feet down a narrow crevice on the side of Brithdir Mountain, near Merthyr Tydfil in Glamorgan. He used only a rope and a ham sandwich. Twenty-seven-year-old Martin Townsend succeeded where other rescuers failed by throwing down the sandwich to lure the hungry dog into a noose he had lowered into the crevice. He then hauled the dog up to the surface.

Local volunteers had removed around 30 tons of rock and earth to get down to within ten feet of the dog, which had fallen down the crevice while chasing rabbits.

Townsend climbed the mountain with a friend after midnight, believing the dog would be easier to catch 'when it was quiet and there was no noise from all the hammer drills that people had been using'. Rocky's owner, 16-year-old Gareth Davies, was delighted to have him back and said the dog was 'a bit thinner, but otherwise great'.

CARDIFF MAN JOSEPH Rapa spent five days in jail in December 1969 because of delays in the Royal Mail. He had posted a weekly instalment on a fine in time, by first-class post, but for some reason it took three days to reach the magistrates' office. By that time a warrant had been posted for Rapa's arrest and he was jailed on 2 December for six days before a court got him out on bail. A judge advised Rapa to petition the Home Secretary when he complained of unfair treatment.

WHAT'S IN A name? On 23 November 1898 the small Porthmadog schooner, *Twelve Apostles*, was wrecked at Hell's Mouth near the tip of the Lleyn peninsula. The *Twelve Apostles* also has another claim to fame. On 7 October 1895 it became the first ship to take a load of slate through the Kiel Canal in Germany.

THE PUBLIC ADVERTISER of 28 October 1814 recounts a remarkable close shave which occurred a short time earlier. A Miss Nicholas was riding along a road overlooking the River Rhymney when her horse took fright, bolted out of control and raced along the road. Ahead, a rock from a cliff had fallen and blocked the road, leaving only a brief gap between the rock and the edge. The horse tried to pass through the space, but its hind legs slipped over the side, leaving only its forelegs on the road. Quick as a flash the girl jumped from the horse, grabbed an overhanging branch and swung to safety, while the horse fell into the waters 200 feet below. It also survived without injury and swam to the opposite bank.

DR STUART DIMOND, a lecturer at University College, Cardiff, disclosed how conservative rats' musical taste was when he spoke to psychology colleagues about his investigations into animal behaviour in September 1970. In the experiment, rats were provided with two pedals. One turned on a recording of Mozart's music, the other played another classical piece by Schoenberg. Dimond said that the rats preferred to play Mozart and concluded that early exposure to classical music had been a significant factor in the experiment. The rats had been reared on a diet of classical music from a young age. From infancy that had been subjected to hearing a complete recording of Mozart's *The Magic Flute*, the fifth violin concerto and two of his symphonies four times a day.

ACCORDING TO THE *Guinness Book of Records* the shortest grass native to Britain is the rare sand bent (*Mibrona minima*) from Anglesey, which grows to a maximum height of less than 6 inches.

FOR TWO MINUTES on 20 March 1987 Sharron Gardiner from Pontypridd, Glamorgan, thought she was the new Miss Wales. Then the MC, Eric Morley, announced that there had been a mix-up, and the 23-year-old receptionist's brief reign ended in tears. The real winner was 18-year-old Nicola Davies. Morley said the official vote-counter had handed him a slip of paper with Sharron's name on it. 'When I announced the result, he suddenly realized he had made a mistake and ran across and handed me the right result', he said.

The unexpected turn of events was a terrible blow for Sharron because she had long dreamed of representing Wales in the Miss Universe contest. The real Miss Wales, Nicola Davies, won a £2,000 prize and a holiday in Greece, while Sharron received £1,000 from the event's organizers as an apology for their blunder.

IN 1892, A CARDIFF boy swallowed fifty-three marbles. Dr J. Thomas later described his case in an issue of *The Lancet*. The boy was admitted to Cardiff Infirmary to be relieved of the marbles. Dr Thomas related that when the youth was turned upside down and shaken, a sound 'like the rattling of a wave receding on a pebbly beach' could be heard. The boy was dosed with a laxative and passed the marbles naturally without having to resort to surgery.

IN 1588 60-YEAR-OLD Margaret Vergh Gryifith from the parish of Llangadfan in Montgomeryshire grew a crooked 4-inch horn out of the centre of her forehead. What little is known about her is from a rare tract published by Thomas

Orwin in London in 1588 which contains a portrait of Margaret. It was published when she moved to London to earn a living exhibiting herself.

SIXTY-YEAR-OLD OWEN JONES from Tyn-y-Gough, Anglesey, filed for divorce in February 1963 on the grounds that his wife had been unfaithful with another man (who was now dead) in 1934.

ACCORDING TO THE gravestone epitaph at Conway Church, Caernarvonshire, Nicholas Hookes, who died in March 1637, was the forty-first child of his mother, Alice Hookes.

IN JULY 2007 Kerry Bevan and Wayne Davies from Wrexham proved just how deep their love was by getting married 500 feet underground in an old slate mine. The couple, together with fifteen guests and a registrar, all wore traditional wedding attire with hard hats and heavy footwear and climbed aboard a battery-powered locomotive to take a 800-metre ride into the heart of the Llechwedd mine in Blaenau Ffestiniog.

A REMARKABLE CHILD prodigy from Glamorgan came to public notice in December 1786 when a brief article in the *Gentleman's Magazine* detailed the astounding mathematical ability of a 10-year-old boy. Thomas John was the son of a labourer from Merthyr Tydfil and could perform extraordinary calculations in his head. His unusual gift came to light when John was only six years old. After hearing a young soldier relate that he had been gone for four years, John corrected him, saying exactly how many days he had been gone. He was found to be correct. A local schoolmaster and other dignitaries tested the boy with complex calculations and he answered correctly each time astounding the men, who readily bore witness to the lad's mathematical prowess.

IN MAY 1988 a 21-year-old Cardiff woman admitted in court that she had committed 2,257 crimes in a four-year crime spree, including the theft of 291 cars and goods worth more than £2 million. She wrote a 37-page confession after talking to police for 165 hours, and was sentenced to 4½ years in prison. She said she stole to support her two children and told the judge, 'I was a very stupid person and I am deeply sorry. I want to get all the crimes cleared up. I want to start afresh.'

ON 14 NOVEMBER 1971 a man with a gun demanded a box from the two bank messengers waiting at a bus stop in Cardiff. One of the men handed him one of the two boxes they were carrying and the gunman sped off. The gunman's box contained the men's lunch. The one left behind held several thousand pounds.

WHEN PORT TALBOT-BORN actor Anthony Hopkins won a role in the film version of George Feifer's *The Girl from Petrovka* in the early 1970s he hunted for a copy of the novel in the bookshops on London's Charing Cross Road. He failed to find a copy and gave up the search. While waiting for a train home at Leicester Square underground station, he noticed a book lying abandoned on a bench. Incredibly, it was a copy of *The Girl from Petrovka*.

Two years later, while filming was underway in Vienna, Feifer visited the set and mentioned that he had no copy of the book himself, having given his last copy to a friend in London, who had then lost it. 'Is this the one,' Hopkins asked, handing him the book, 'with notes scribbled in the margins?' Amazingly, it was Feifer's long-lost annotated copy.

TRAINEE TEACHER VANIA LUCCHESI was inundated with requests for interviews in October 2001 when a newspaper revealed how she had accidentally swallowed a 7-inch-long pink toothbrush at her home in Cathays, Cardiff. 'I was in a hurry and brushing the teeth at the back of my mouth', she explained. 'I missed the step in the bathroom, my neck went back and I gasped with fright. I could feel the brush in my windpipe. It felt painful and I was scared, and then it slipped down into my stomach.'

Vania was alone in the flat at the time. Instead of dialling 999 for an ambulance she rang a taxi to take her to the University Hospital of Wales. In Casualty, she explained what had happened and X-rays showed the brush lodged in her stomach. Doctors tried to hook the toothbrush, using a miniature endoscope camera, but the attempt failed and it was deemed safer to make a small incision in Vania's stomach and remove it surgically. After the successful operation, the toothbrush was returned to

Vania, who planned to keep it as a souvenir. The one good thing to come out of the accident was that she pledged to donate any appearance fees to the Noah's Ark Appeal to build a children's hospital in Wales.

REGULAR DRINKERS AT the pub John Wearn managed liked him so much that they bricked up the pub's door to stop him from moving to another job. 'I was fuming at first but now I can see the funny side. It was drastic action on their part, but it's nice to feel wanted', Wearn said. The customers of the Great Western Hotel in Edwardsville, Glamorgan bricked up Wearn's door after closing time on 20 June 1986. One regular drinker explained: 'It was a spur-of-the-moment thing, but at first John was not amused. He's a great landlord who keeps a good pint, so we don't want him to leave the pub.'

ON 16 JULY 1969, a Cardiff jury found a policeman innocent of stealing 47 daffodils worth 5 shillings while on night patrol on the grounds of Cardiff Castle. The officer claimed that he had found the flowers strewn on a river-bank and that he had not picked them in the castle gardens, as charged.

IN 1761 FOUR Welsh women walked from the foot of Westminster Bridge to the Boot and Crown, over Deptford Bridge, and back again in an hour and three-quarters, for a bet of £20. They had been allowed two and a half hours to complete the wager.

In January 1970 the Empire Bingo and Social Club in Barry, Glamorgan, offered a gentleman as a prize for the lady who won its grand bingo prize. Tyrone Francis, a 20-year-old six-footer, who was the prize, said that for twenty-four hours he would do everything the winner says –'anything short of murder'.

Welshman Samuel Evens, a private grenadier in the Second Regiment of Foot, died in the Military Hospital in Plymouth, Devon, on 30 January 1809, sixteen days after he had been shot through the heart. For many years his preserved heart was on display at the hospital.

Patrick Mevel's neighbours could no longer stand the smell coming from his Cardiff apartment in November 1983 and called in the city inspectors, who found tons of onions stored from floor to ceiling in three of the four apartment's rooms. Mevel, a native of Brittany, would don a beret and sell his onions on the streets of Cardiff.

Ann Sage from Bridgend, Glamorgan, suffered from physical pain and mental anguish for three years before doctors discovered the cause of her problems. Doctors had begun to think her debilitating pain was psychosomatic until she insisted on having an X-ray and a 2½-cm-long sewing needle was discovered lodged in her groin. The 43-year-old mother of two did not know how long the needle had been there, but she thought it may have entered her body when she was eleven as she had injured herself bouncing on an old mattress. Ann underwent a three-hour operation at Llandough Hospital in Cardiff in June 2001 to have the needle removed. The operation was a success and Ann's health rapidly improved.

Jane Clemence from Canton, Cardiff, suffered from a similar problem for eight years, putting up with 'a painful tingle' in her right thigh. Again the doctors could not find the cause of the problem until one finally agreed to take an X-ray. A 2-inch needle was found. Jane underwent minor surgery to remove it in April 1993. 'I was beginning to doubt myself', she said. 'Whenever I tried to describe the pain, I said it was like pins and needles or like a pin sticking in my leg.'

IN MAY 1988 a 6-year-old summoned help for stranded holidaymakers after riding piggyback on the shoulders of a deaf-mute man in a 100-foot climb up a cliff. A group of ten adults, two children and two dogs were on a beach at the foot of a cliff on the Penarth coast in Glamorgan when an incoming tide stranded them. Six-foot-tall Alan Thomas volunteered to make the climb, but because he could neither hear nor speak, he carried Sara Reinhardt on his back to seek help at a camping ground near the cliff-top. The others huddled together on a ledge and were rescued after Sara had found help.

A CARDIFF SOLDIER regained his speech in January 1915 after his mother heroically threw herself down the stairs in a bid to shock him into speaking again. Corporal Tucker was injured at the first Battle of Ypres in late 1914 and was so shaken by his experiences, he was unable to talk. He was sent home to recuperate, but remained unable to talk until his mother purposely fell down the stairs while he was visiting her.

When he heard her tumbling down, Tucker rushed to the hallway and, finding her lying at the bottom of the stairs groaning, he called out 'Oh, Mother' and fainted. 'When I recovered, I found my mother, cool and smiling, holding my head, while I was crying', he said. 'In my weak and nervous condition, the shock was too much. I then learned she had deliberately fallen, and bruised herself badly in doing so. My nerves are still in bad shape, but when they are well I hope to return to duty again at the Front.'

AFTER FINISHING A shift at the Oakdale Colliery near Blackwood, Monmouthshire, in September 1942, young miner Ronald Cutler blew his nose to get rid of the coal dust that was clogging it. To Cutler's astonishment, his eye fell out! Ambulance men replaced the eye and Cutler was later able to go home. He appeared none the worse for wear after the bizarre accident and his eye remained fully functioning, though it needed further treatment.

IN MAY 1986 45-year-old Pamela Harris from Pontypridd, Glamorgan, felt what she thought was just a bad case of stomach cramp while she was in her bathroom. Then she gave birth to a 3 lb 10 oz boy. She had had no idea that she was pregnant.

IN WALES THERE are many documented instances of strange objects falling from the sky. One such case comes from the village of Mountain Ash in Glamorgan. At 11 a.m. on 9 February 1859 a large number of small live fish fell on the fields and houses during a heavy storm. There were two falls about ten minutes apart and the event was witnessed by many people. Two local clergymen collected eyewitness accounts to preserve testimony about the curious event. One of the remarkable statements came from local man John Lewis, who worked as a sawyer:

> I was getting out a piece of timber, for the purpose of setting it for the saw, when I was startled by something falling all over me – down my neck, on my head, and on my back. On putting my hand down my neck, I was surprised to find they were little fish. By this time I saw the whole ground covered with them. I took off my hat, the brim of which was full of them. They were jumping all about. They covered the ground in a long strip of about 80 yards by 12, as we measured afterwards. That shed was covered with them, and the shoots were quite full of them. My mate and I might have gathered bucketsful of them, scraping with our hands. We did gather a great many, about a bucketful, and threw them into the rain pool, where some of them now are. There were two showers with an interval of about ten minutes, and each shower lasted about two minutes or thereabouts. The morning up-train to Aberdare was just then passing. It was not blowing very hard,

but uncommon wet; just about the same wind as there is today, and it came from this quarter. They came down with the rain in a body, like.

The largest fish, 5 inches long, died soon after being found, but most ranged in size from 1–4 inches. The local curate sent a report to *The Times* (2 March 1859) which stated that the locals tried to save the fish by putting them in salt water and fresh water. Only those placed in fresh water survived. Specimens were sent to the British Museum, where Dr John Gray, Keeper of Zoology, identified them as minnows and sticklebacks.

IT WAS A sports commentator's nightmare on 5 May 1988 when Gordon Brand played Gordon Brand while David Russell was paired with David Russell in the second round of the £280,000 Grand Prix of Europe matchplay golf championship at Chepstow, Monmouthshire. Neither of the pair of namesakes were related to each other. When the players squared off around St Pierre Golf and Country Club course to decide which Gordon Brand and David Russell would advance to the third round, the results were as follows: Englishman Gordon J. Brand defeated Scotsman Gordon Brand Jr 2 and 1, while David J. Russell defeated fellow Englishman David A. Russell 1-up.

THE *ANNUAL REGISTER* for 1759 records that on 18 October of that year, Evan Price of Dolgellau, Merionethshire, died aged 120, adding that up to a month before his death 'he used to walk 4 miles twice a week, in that hilly country'.

ERIC KINSELLA FROM Cwmbran, Monmouthshire, was furious in May 1964 when a doctor ruled that he was 'unfit' to work as a machine operator for an engineering firm because he had too much hair on his chest.

ON 20 JULY 1827, half a ton of hay was seen sailing overhead into the wind by field-workers in Denbighshire. As the hay went past, a few wisps fluttered down on the surprised workers.

THE RSPCA WAS alerted in November 1992 when worried onlookers became concerned about an owl that had perched on a pylon at Johnstown, near Wrexham, and never flew away. An RSPCA official spent nearly an hour trying to coax the owl down before a local told him he was wasting his time because the 'bird' was a decoy, made of wood, placed there by the electricity company to discourage any nest-building on the site.

ROY CALLOWAY FROM Usk in Monmouthshire was amazed to discover that he had been living with a broken leg for fifty years. The 70-year-old retired steelworker had suffered multiple fractures in his right leg in a motorbike crash in 1958. He spent six months in hospital and two years on crutches before being able to walk again, but still remained in pain. In 2008 the pain worsened and Calloway was sent for an X-ray, which revealed that his leg bones had never knitted back together properly. 'It was a shock to find the leg was still broken, but it explains a lot', he said. 'I've been in pain for nearly half a century, but I don't want surgery because I'm scared I might lose my leg.'

SIGNS OF STRANGE TIMES, a broadsheet published in London in 1681, records that on 12 September 1680 a naval battle in the sky was witnessed by a clergyman and several other people near Porsnet in Monmouthshire. One fleet came from the north, the other from the south. A great ship fired first, 'and after her, the rest discharged their vollies in order, so that great flashings of fire, and even smoak was visible, and noises in the ayr as of great guns'. After this, a phantom aerial battle took place in 'a square medow' near Porsnet, accompanied by the sounds of war and the cries of the injured and dying.

THE RENT PAID for the 147-acre Waterton Farm, near Coity, Bridgend, Glamorgan, was once fixed at only ¼ lb of pepper, which the landlord had to collect each year on or around midsummer in a cart drawn by eight white oxen.

A PARK GARDENER'S assistant in Newport went on a rampage in August 1952 after being driven half-mad by flowerpots. Instead of gardening, the 15-year-old's job was the monotonous task of washing flowerpots all day long, which he came to hate. The final straw came when people started calling him 'pot washer' while he was out with his girlfriend. In a fury, the youth rampaged through the potting shed and broke the stems of 328 prize chrysanthemums valued at £125. Then he left a note calling his employer a 'pig-headed slave driver'. In the youth's defence, his counsel pleaded that he 'had gone berserk'. The Newport juvenile court fined the pot-hater £5.

ON 16 JUNE 1884 immense swarms of caterpillars were reported to have made their appearance in the mountainous district of east Glamorgan, especially between the Greater Rhondda Valley and Maesteg. The insects were brown, with black longitudinal stripes and were about 1½ inches long. Millions of them devastated a ten-mile stretch of land.

WALES GAS BOARD chairman T. Mervyn Jones went personally to Mrs Evelyn Brokenshire's Cardiff home on 10 June 1974 to apologize for overcharging her on her gas bill. Mrs Brokenshire had complained that her bill, which should have been £2.50, read £250. Jones explained that the mistake was made by a new £100,000 computer installed to save time and manpower.

THE *GENTLEMAN'S MAGAZINE* for 1749 records an unusual phenomenon that occurred at Milford Haven, Pembrokeshire, on 2 July of that year. Near low tide at 11 a.m., the sea was smooth and the weather was calm one minute, then the inhabitants became alarmed at 'a sudden hideous rumbling of the water'. To the spectators' amazement the sea rushed up to the high water mark in less than a minute, then fell back just as quickly. This happened seven more times over the next forty-five minutes. The sudden rushing of water was so violent that boats were forced from their moorings and thrown about like toys. Fortunately, no lives were lost.

A BATTLE OF wits took place in Machynlleth, Montgomeryshire in late 1972. Each time council workers sprinkled poisonous powder on the streets to try to kill pigeons, 69-year-old Edith Vaughan swept it up. 'The town council is taking legal advice to try and stop me,' she said, 'but I will keep right on doing it. It's cruel.'

IN THE WELSH sport of 'purring', two persons face each other with their hands on each other's shoulders, then begin kicking each other in the shins with heavy boots. The first person to let go of his opponent's shoulders loses.

ON NOVEMBER 1990, 11-year-old Ryan Fleet from Blackwood, Monmouthshire, found a 9 mm bullet between two slices of bread he was buttering. A serious accident could easily have occurred because Ryan's mother Jenny usually froze loaves of bread and then defrosted them in a microwave when they were needed. If she had done that to this loaf, the bullet would have exploded. It is not known how the bullet came to be inside the loaf. The white sliced and wrapped loaf had come from a Spar supermarket in nearby Cefn Fforest and was thought to have been baked in Bristol.

SOME 4,900 POLICE and soldiers were on hand in Caernarvon to provide security for visiting dignitaries attending Prince Charles's investiture as the twenty-first Prince of Wales at Caernarvon Castle on 1 July 1969. Following a bomb explosion in a post office in Cardiff the day before, security forces were on edge and one policeman was so nervous that he even asked Princess Margaret, one of the best-known faces in the world, to show her pass and so prove her identity.

TREGARON BOG IN Cardiganshire is the only habitat of the rare British Black Adder.

ON 14 JUNE 1964 night telephonist William Michael from Neath prevented a robbery when he plugged in a call on his switchboard and heard a frightened woman ask 'What do you want, boys?' The line went dead and Michael alerted police, who captured the thieves.

LEWIS EVAN MORGAN from Gwyllgyth in Glamorgan died aged ninety-eight in 1798. He left a generous will, along with a backhanded compliment in a few neat sentences that get straight to the point: 'I give to my faithful servant, Esther Jones, the whole that I am possessed of either in personal property, land, or otherwise. She is a tolerable good woman, but would be much better if she had not so clamorous a tongue. She has, however, one great virtue, which is a veil to all her foibles – strict honesty.'

LETTERS POSTED IN Neath, Glamorgan, in mid-February 1964 arrived at their destination long before they were officially sent. A new clerk at the post office made an error fixing the postmark stamp. To make matters worse, he used the date 30 February.

THE FOLLOWING WEDDING invitation was published in the *Cumberland Pacquet* newspaper in 1836 and is quite typical of the period:

> Carmarthen, April 12, 1836
>
> As we intend to enter the MATRIMONIAL STATE on Thursday, the 15th of MAY next, we are encouraged by our Friends to make a BIDDING on the occasion the same Day, at the Sign of the Angel, situated in LAMMAS-STREET; when and where the favour of your good and agreeable Company is most humbly solicited, and whatever donation you may be pleased to confer on us then, will be thankfully received, warmly encouraged, and cheerfully repaid whenever called for on a similar occasion,
>
> By your most obedient humble Servants,
> DAVID DANIEL
> (Shoemaker)
> RUTH EVANS.

A SWANSEA TEACHER preparing lunch for her sixteen pupils in a primary school in October 1966 mistook rat poison for oatmeal and sprinkled it generously on a rice pudding dessert. Luckily, the pudding turned blue and the children refused to eat it.

In July 1963 it was revealed that Miss Ada Tilley from Aberdaron, Caernarvonshire, left all but £140 of her £182,000 estate for the treatment of sick cats. A niece who had cared for the elderly woman for the last eight years of her life was not a beneficiary of the will.

One of the most celebrated skeletons of a human who had lived was that of Hopkins Hopkins from Llantrisant, Glamorgan, who was only 2 feet 6 inches tall and never weighed more than 17 lb during his short life. It was exhibited as a freak of nature in Wales and London. In the three years before his death in March 1754, at the age of seventeen, his weight is said to have remained around 12 lb.

It is said that he died of 'mere old age and a gradual decay of nature'. Most likely the unfortunate youth suffered from progeria, an extremely rare genetic condition. Sufferers literally die of old age before they are out of their teens. Hopkins's parents had six other children, all of whom were healthy, apart from a 10-year-old girl, who weighed only 18 lb and was rapidly ageing like her brother at the time of his death.

Nigel Blundell's book *The World's Greatest Mistakes* (1980) contains a brief paragraph describing the cruel twist of fate that happened to Victor Grant from Wrexham. Grant had been saving up for a new car to surprise his wife and had already collected £500 and hidden it in a bundle of old clothes. One day, while he was at work, his wife put them out with the rubbish. When he arrived home, Grant discovered what his wife had done and hired a digger to try to find his money in the local rubbish dump. After two days' searching he gave up and started saving again. This time, he planned to put his money in a bank.

ON 2 OCTOBER 1992, historian and writer Jan Morris answered the telephone at home in Llanystumdwy, Caernarvonshire, and received a pleasant surprise. Without introducing themselves, a man and a woman sang 'Happy Birthday to You' to Morris – well, to someone called Denis. They had dialled the wrong number. However, it also happened to be Jan Morris's birthday.

ACCORDING TO THE *Guinness Book of Records*, the most prolific user of any suggestion box scheme is John Drayton (1907–87) of Newport, who submitted an incredible 31,400 suggestions to British railway authorities from 1924 to August 1987. Drayton had a remarkable success rate – one in seven of his suggestions were adopted. As a special tribute for his years of making suggestions, British Rail presented Drayton with a chiming clock in 1983.

IN 2003 LOIS JONES from Pentrecelyn, near Ruthin, Denbighshire, had the shock of her life when the stranger she met by accident in Sydney, Australia, turned out to be her sister's boyfriend. Lois was staying in a youth hostel, but her swipe card would not work to allow her to enter it. She asked the first person – a male – who came along for help. When he heard her accent and discovered that she was from Ruthin, he remarked that his girlfriend, Non, came from there. It quickly emerged that he was her sister's boyfriend, Alex Jones from Sheffield. Lois and Alex had never met before because she had been living away from home when he had visited Non. This was not the only coincidence Lois encountered in Australia. In Alice Springs she was approached by a Welsh couple, who asked her for directions. It turned out the man had been in college with Lois's father.

THE LAST FATAL duel to be fought in Wales took place at Dan-warin fields between Llandyfyriog and Adpar in Cardiganshire on 10 September 1814, when John Benyon shot John Heslop after an argument at the Old Salutation Inn at Adpar. Heslop was fatally wounded and died shortly afterwards. He was buried at nearby Llandyfyriog churchyard where a tombstone with the inscription containing the line 'Alas, poor Heslop' can still be seen.

IN JUNE 1965 a neon sign stretching for a quarter of a mile was installed over Cardiff's new fruit and vegetable market. It was believed to be the longest of its kind in the world.

WILLIAM BONVIL OF Pwllywrach, Glamorgan, went out to sea fishing with a few friends in early August 1765 and netted several fish. In order to stop one small fish slipping out of his hands, Bonvil gripped it with his teeth (a common practice among fishermen). Unfortunately, the fish wriggled and slipped into his throat. Since the scales had anchored the fish in his throat, it could not be pulled out and Bonvil choked to death in just a minute or so.

SWANSEA JACK WAS a black Labrador retriever belonging to William Thomas from the North Dock area of Swansea. The dog was famous for saving twenty-seven people from drowning near the docks. Jack's first rescue took place in June 1931 when he saved a 12-year-old boy who was in difficulty, by diving into the water and pulling him to safety at the dockside. Swansea Jack's heroism was widely acknowledged and he received several awards. He died in October 1937 aged seven, after eating rat poison. There is a memorial to this remarkable dog at the Promenade near St Helen's Rugby Ground in Swansea.

DR DICK VAN STEENIS from Cwmgwrach in Glamorgan had to close his surgery office in September 1966 because all the villagers were using it as a public meeting place, 'to chat with their neighbours'.

ONE OF THE strangest finds made underground in a coal mine was a badly injured parrot. The bird was found 500 feet down the Celynen North mine in Ebbw Vale, Monmouthshire, in May 1984.

ACCORDING TO THE *Guinness Book of Records*, the smallest house in Britain is a nineteenth-century fisherman's cottage on The Quay in Conway, Caernarvonshire. This tiny dwelling has a street frontage of just 6 feet. It is 10 feet 2 inches high and measures just 8 feet 4 inches from back to front. It has two tiny rooms and a staircase. Its last inhabitant was 6 feet, 3 inches tall.

WILLIAM GEORGE (1865–1967), brother of Prime Minister David Lloyd George, passed his law exams in May 1880 and was still practising as a solicitor in December 1966, aged 101 years and 9 months.

WHEN 13-YEAR-OLD GRAHAM WARD began pedalling the new organ at Jerusalem Congregational Church in Llanberis, Caernarvonshire, in October 1964, he knew it did not sound right. On investigating, he discovered a biscuit tin full of money – £1,360 to be exact. Church officials said an elderly lady had donated the organ to the church when the old one had broken down. Her money was returned.

A JURY OF ten men and two women was accidentally locked into a cell in a Cardiff prison in February 1971 while inspecting a prosecution claim that two defendants had been overheard discussing a bank raid of which they stood accused. The jurors were freed after about ten minutes.

WHEN THE THOUGHTFUL wife of Richard Hughes, a robber, met her husband on his way to his execution at London's Tyburn on 24 June 1709, she whispered, 'My dear, who must find the rope that is to hang you – me or the sheriff?' Hughes, from Betws, Denbighshire, replied: 'The sheriff, honey; for who's obliged to find him tools to do his work?' 'Ah!', replied his wife, 'I wish I had known so much before; it would have saved me twopence, for I have been and bought one already.' 'Well, well,' said Hughes cheerfully, 'perhaps it mayn't be lost. It may serve a second husband!' 'Yes,' she said, 'if I have any luck in good husbands, so it may.'

THE *SPORTING MAGAZINE* of April 1794 relates an unusual incident which happened to 'Mr Roche's Foxhounds' in Pembrokeshire. On a thick foggy day, some of Roche's best hounds were lost in the Hook Wood. Despite an extensive search and the offer of a considerable reward, they were not found. About three weeks later a collier heard a noise coming from a nearby pit. He got a rope and climbed down to find one bitch alive and in good condition. He also found the skulls of the other foxhounds and a smaller one, like a fox's head, all picked to the bone, along with the one remaining uneaten hind quarter.

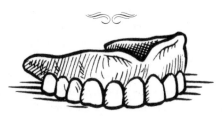

TOWYN IN MERIONETH has been an unlucky place for people named Jones who had false teeth. William L. Jones was enjoying a dip in the sea near Towyn in September 1934 when a wave took him by surprise and his false teeth popped out and disappeared. Four days later the police informed him that the missing teeth had been washed ashore.

When Griffith Jones and his four sons pulled up their net while fishing off Towyn in late November 1938, an upper set of false teeth was among their haul of fish. They were a pair lost by another William Jones while he had been holidaying in the town.

A BIZARRE ACCIDENT occurred on 29 October 1772, verified by eyewitnesses. At the time, a wooden bridge spanned the River Usk at Caerleon in Monmouthshire and was liable to be carried away when the river flooded. Anne Williams was returning home at around eleven o'clock at night when a violent surge smashed into the bridge while she was crossing it and bore away a large piece of the bridge with her on it. The wreckage remained intact and Anne had the presence of mind to cling to the railing and scream for help.

People living along the river heard her cries, but the fast current carried her away before help could reach her.

The bridge section was smashed to pieces against one of the piers of Newport bridge. Fortunately, Anne managed to straddle a beam and remain safe. The bridge piece was slowed by eddies around the bridge and gave Anne hope that she might be rescued there. Then, without warning, the beam was swept down the river. Anne resigned herself to being carried out to sea, but about a mile from Newport she saw a flickering light in a barge near the shore and redoubled her cries.

She was heard by the barge-master, who jumped into a boat with one of his men and rowed after Anne down the violent river. He shouted at Anne to remain calm and to stay on the beam. It was so dark, neither party could see the other, but at last the men caught up with the poor woman and had lashed the beam to the boat fore and aft when the cloudy night sky suddenly cleared. The men heaved Anne aboard, but by the time they had disentangled the boat from the beam, they had almost reached the mouth of the Usk. They rowed to shore and rested until dawn, then brought Anne to Newport. She was four months' pregnant, but after a few hours' rest she felt well enough to return to Caerleon.

On 21 March 1773 Anne Williams gave birth to a boy and called him John. The entry in the birth register of St Cadoc's Church in Caerleon adds he was 'remarkable for his own and mother's miraculous deliverance'.

AN UNUSUAL CONFLICT took place in Lampeter, Cardiganshire, on 11 March 1810. Two elderly women, one aged eighty-eight, the other eighty-six, who had been friends for nearly sixty years, argued over a hank of yarn, which the younger accused the elder of stealing from her. After some sharp words, they came to blows. Their anger was greater than their strength and they called it a draw in order that they might fight it out with cudgels the following day. The bellman proclaimed the combat throughout the town.

After the women beat each other 'most unmercifully', the magistrates intervened and put an end to the duel. There had been nearly an hour's 'hard fighting' and the younger octogenarian seemed to have the advantage. If the fight had not been broken up, she would certainly have killed her antagonist, who nonetheless had never called for quarter.

REVEREND PEREGRINE PHILLIPS (1623–91) from Amroth, Pembrokeshire, had a close escape from death a few years before his actual demise. He was riding home late one night near Freystrup, where there were a large number of coal-pits, when he and his horse fell into a very deep one, half-full of water. The pit narrowed considerably some twenty feet below the surface and the horse stuck fast, with its rider still on it. Fortunately for the Reverend, an old deaf woman was travelling that way with her grandchild. The child heard a cry for help and with great difficulty persuaded her grandmother to see what it was. They found Phillips's precarious situation and got help. The curate suffered no serious injuries.

WILLIAM LEWIS WAS buried at New Radnor in Radnorshire in September 1882, having died aged 101. As well as having lived to a great age, he must have remained in remarkable health. At the age of eighty-five he went to America, but did not stay there long. At ninety-five, it is said that Lewis walked from New Radnor to Knighton and back in one day – a distance of twenty miles.

IN HER 1877 book *Memorials of Charlotte Williams-Wynn*, the eponymous diarist recorded a curious anecdote:

> Llangedwyn, Sep, 1843. My Cousin is now here, and has brought over nearly two hundred hounds to hunt some wretched foxes which are supposed to be in the woods. I proposed to him to take a gun and shoot them to save time, but he was quite horrified at the idea, so the whole valley has been disturbed this morning by the howling and screeching of these beasts, and the glorious result has been three little foxes, to accomplish which he had to be out at four o'clock in the morning.

A BOY DESCRIBED in handbills as 'the Welsh Porcupine Youth' was exhibited across Britain in the early 1840s. The *Salopian Journal* of 24 February 1841 contains a paragraph informing readers that he was being exhibited at Oswestry and reported 'his lively conversation and interesting features contrast sharply with the horny excrescences with which his limbs and other parts of his body are covered and render him at once an object of great attraction and sympathy'.

Writing forty years later, one man recalled being taken as a child to see the boy in a local public house in a Glamorgan village:

I have a vivid recollection of the scene, although from the number of people who were crowded into the room, I did not see as much of him as I desired. He was a lively little fellow of about six or seven years old, and talked very fluent Welsh to those in charge of him. On this particular occasion he had been rather fretful, many persons having called to see him during the preceding afternoon, and he had to be kept amused. His father and an uncle travelled about with him and looked like young men from the Colliery districts out for a holiday. I think he was called the 'Hedgehog Boy' on this occasion. He was shown as sitting on somebody's lap, without much clothing; and his skin was indeed remarkable. It was not of uniform roughness, but much of it looked like hedgehog's prickles – the thighs and shoulders especially.

DAVID WILSON WAS born on the Banwen Mountain near Glynneath, Glamorganshire, in 1846 and is remarkable for a string of unlucky incidents that happened to him. A coal-miner by profession, Wilson set a record for the number of accidents he had suffered on the same day of the year. On 26 August 1857, at the age of ten, he fractured the forefinger of his right hand. Two years later, again on 26 August, he fell from a horse and broke his left leg below the knee. On the same date the next year he broke both bones of his left forearm by stumbling and hitting his arm of the edge of a brick.

On 26 August 1861, Wilson, now fourteen, again broke his left leg above the ankle when his foot caught under an iron rod, his body pitching forwards. The next 26 August he suffered his worst accident yet, breaking both his legs. The right one was injured so badly, it had to be amputated. This accident was caused by a horse running away underground when hitched to a tram of coal. It caught Wilson in a narrow passage and crushed both his legs.

By now Wilson had had five accidents in six years, all on the same date. He resolved never again to work on 26 August. He managed to do this for twenty-eight years, but in 1890 he forgot the date and went to work as usual. He broke his remaining (left) leg for the fourth time when part of the roof on a tunnel he was working on at Risca Colliery fell in. Wilson resolved not to work on 26 August ever again. He was interviewed at the turn of the century and gave an upbeat account of his life, proudly showing off the many scars he had gathered from his accidents. He was still working at the colliery and was in rude health.

IN OCTOBER 1805 a deer was being hunted at Llantrithyd, Glamorgan, but managed to evade its pursuers by jumping into the sea. It swam more than two miles and escaped capture.

IN THE SUMMER of 1828 a Caernarvonshire gentleman was invited to stay a month with a friend in Middlewich, Cheshire. He took a favourite pet greyhound with him. The day after their arrival, their host's mastiff dog attacked the greyhound and 'gave him a good drubbing'. The greyhound immediately took to his heels and fled back to his home in upper Caernarvonshire, ninety miles away. His arrival and wonderful homing instinct astonished his owner's family. The next morning they discovered that the greyhound and the family's bull mastiff dog had disappeared. Neither of them could be found. A few days later a letter arrived from their owner in Middlewich. The two dogs had turned up there and had attacked and killed his host's mastiff dog, before they could be stopped.

DURING A HEAVY rainstorm on 13 August 1890 tens of thousands of small frogs fell from the sky onto Holway Road, just outside Holywell in Flintshire. For a distance of 200 yards the road was covered with the little creatures.

IN THE NOVEMBER 1913 issue of the *Strand Magazine* there is a photograph illustrating a phenomenon visible only in the tropics: sunshine at noon where no shadow is cast by objects exposed to the sun's rays, the explanation being that the ship was photographed at the exact time of the sun's peak. This phenomenon was recorded by Captain W.M. Gibbs of Cardiff in latitude 14 degrees south in February 1913. He had previously witnessed the same phenomenon in 1881 at about the same time of year in practically the same latitude.

This was not the only coincidence to have occurred in Captain Gibbs's life. On New Year's Eve 1898 the captain realized that his ship was in precisely the same spot as she had been at midnight on New Year's Eve the year before. Shocked by the coincidence, Gibbs got his chief mate to check the ship's position, which was some thirty miles off the coast of Algiers. He concurred with the captain and the crew toasted the wonderful coincidence.

JOHN PARRY (c. 1710–82) from Ruabon, Denbighshire, was born blind. Despite this handicap, he learned to master the Welsh triple harp from an early age and was renowned as a celebrated harpist. He was also an excellent draughts player, one of the finest of his time.

THE *GENTLEMAN'S MAGAZINE* of June 1820 carries a description of an enormous hollow oak tree on the estate of C.H. Leigh near Pontypool in Monmouthshire. During the winter a tenant of Leigh's usually reared six or seven calves inside it. The tree was so large that two people on horseback could ride into it, turn and go out again without dismounting. Frustratingly, the article does not give the dimensions of this great oak.

Another issue of the same magazine for September 1811 does give some measurements for another giant oak nearing the end of its life. It grew at Hendre, near Denbigh, in the farmyard of Reverend W. Chambers. At its base the oak was 33 feet in circumference and it was 30 feet in circumference 15 feet from the ground. Only one branch had foliage and it is said that the 'venerable trunk forms a pig-stye capable of accommodating near a score of the swinish multitude'.

SOME FISHERMEN FROM Angle in Pembrokeshire were proceeding in a boat on 10 August 1876 to visit their lobster pots in West Angle Bay when they spotted a shorthorn cow on an inaccessible beach beneath the high cliffs of Studdock Farm. They concluded that the animal must have fallen over the cliff, but when they reached her, the cow was uninjured. They took her in tow by a rope attached to the boat and rowed to a small bay near Thorn Island fort. The 'sea cow' did not belong to anyone in the area and her origin was a mystery. One thing was certain: if the animal had not been rescued she would have drowned at high tide in the bay.

The puzzle concerning the cow's origin was soon solved. On the morning of 10 August the steamer *Vulture* arrived at Neyland from Waterford in Ireland with a cargo of cattle and other stock. When the animals were unloaded, it was discovered that a cow was missing. The 'sea cow' was identified as the missing animal because she was branded with her owner's initials. Nobody knew how the cow had gone overboard. She either jumped or was lifted by other animals through a doorway, left open for ventilation, and must have swum a great distance.

JOHN EVANS FROM Llanidloes, Montgomeryshire, bought a pony from William Thomas of Five Roads, Llanelli in October 1909. On 23 October the pony was found in the road near his old master's house, having found his way home over a distance of nearly eighty miles.

THE SKOMER VOLE (*Myodes glareolus skomerensis*) is found nowhere else in the world except on the island of Skomer in Pembrokeshire. It is a subspecies of bank vole and probably arrived on the island sometime after the last Ice Age. At under 5 inches long and weighing less than 1½ oz, the Skomer Vole is a small but hardy rodent. Despite its short lifespan of a year and a half, the species thrives on the island. It is estimated that there are around 20,000 voles on Skomer.

AROUND 1815 OWEN Williams of Bodedern, Anglesey, suddenly lost his sight and was left completely blind. Forty years later, Williams, now ninety-two, was sitting by the fireside when his sight suddenly returned. Although shocked, he was delighted to see again after so many years of total blindness.

A TERRIBLE EVENT occurred at Porth in the Rhondda Valley in Glamorganshire on the afternoon of 29 December 1894. Mrs Catherine Bowden was walking along Bridge Street when the earth suddenly opened, and she disappeared. Terrified eyewitnesses ignored the danger and rushed to the spot to try to save her. There was no sign of Mrs Bowden – only a cave 30 feet deep – but they could hear her cries for help. A collier named Jones was lowered into the hole to rescue the poor woman, but the rope snapped, and he too disappeared. Another man named Rogers managed to rescue Jones and Mrs Bowden. She was only slightly injured, but poor Jones died.

SIR JOHN PRYCE (c. 1698–1761) of Newtown Hall, Montgomeryshire, was a very eccentric man. He kept the embalmed bodies of his first two wives in his bedroom, on either side of his bed. They were buried only when the woman who was to become his third wife insisted that her predecessors' corpses be decently interred.

After the death of his second wife, Pryce wrote to the curate of Newtown, then on his deathbed, to ask the clergyman to deliver messages of affection to both his wives in heaven, and to ask the second to appear to him. When his third wife died, Pryce invited a well-known faith-healer of the day, Bridget Bostock, the 'Cheshire Pythoness', to bring her back to life. The attempt was unsuccessful.

FOR A SMALL wager, a barber and a gentleman's servant ran on foot over a distance of a mile against each other at Haverfordwest racecourse in October 1805. The servant, though heavily built, was obliged to carry an extra 84 lb of deadweight to match the barber's weight. For most of the race the barber led, but as they neared the finish line the gentleman's servant dashed by his opponent and won the race.

THE FOLLOWING CURIOUS letter was written on 12 February 1797 by William Pries, who was a surgeon from Llangurig, Montgomeryshire:

> This is To Certify that this Richd Massor was under My hand of a great bruse on his spine and that did gather To a Hydrops and was Torbed and I think that he is not fit To Serve the Militia, for he is not free from that complaint Now he Did hurt the Rines and it very Bad on the Change of the Weather. From y. Willm Pries, Surgeon.

AFTER DELIVERING VEGETABLES to Parkgate in Cheshire on 17 September 1819, an old man attempted to return home to Flint across the sands after dark. Unfortunately he mistook the signal light down the river for one usually placed on the Flint shore and, before he knew it, his horse went into the centre of the River Dee. His pitiful cries for help were heard at Parkgate, and four brave men with lanterns risked their lives to search for him.

After going some two or three miles on the sands and wading through deep gullies formed by the incoming tide, they saw the horse's tracks and ultimately found the exhausted old man just as the water was beginning to float him and the horse. He was lying with his face along the horse's neck, too weak to cry out for help, praying, after giving up all hope of rescue. They seized the bridle and soon brought him safely ashore to Parkgate, where he soon recovered.

HUNDREDS OF PEOPLE witnessed the novel sight of an angry whale towing a small boat full of terrified men in the Menai Straits on 9 December 1883. Local man John Williams had discovered a 14-foot whale stranded on the beach below the Anglesey Arms Hotel at Menai Bridge. He and some friends then attacked the poor creature with pocket knives to try to kill it. The whale bled so profusely that the water turned red for yards around with its blood. Although beached, the whale was dangerous to approach and thrashed violently as it lay helpless and in agony.

Despite this, Williams and his friends tied a rope around the whale's shoulder and fastened it to a boat. When the tide returned, the whale freed itself and took off at speed, towing the boat and its four occupants, who were terrified at this unexpected turn of events. The whale proceeded up the Straits at great speed, then turned sharply at the railway bridge and coursed down the Straits again.

The boat nearly capsized several times and the men clung on for dear life. Finally the stricken creature made for land and beached itself again at a spot close to where it had been found. This time the whale was dragged out of the water's reach and it died soon afterwards. The short but perilous boat ride greatly entertained the gathered crowds and gave the four men an experience to remember for the rest of their days.

CAPTAIN THOMPSON OF the steamer *Muley Hassan* was presented with a silver medal at Cardiff Town Hall on 29

July 1887 for saving a man's life. The steamer was passing through the Straits of Gibraltar, when the captain's retriever dog showed signs of restlessness and eventually jumped overboard. A boat was lowered and the dog was discovered holding a collar of the coat of a drowning man, who was lying across two oars. The man was the only survivor of a Spanish ship which had sunk four hours previously.

FOR A WAGER of 100 guineas, in May 1702 Welshman John Morgan undertook to walk from London to Land's End in Cornwall and back again (612 miles) in fourteen days. He accomplished this with nine hours to spare.

IN JANUARY 1794 two men took advantage of a heavy snowfall at Welshpool, Montgomeryshire, to go hunting. They discovered the tracks of a rabbit and followed them for nearly two hours. The hunters were so certain they would catch the rabbit, they argued over who would get to keep it when they killed it. Just as they caught up to their intended prey, a young fox appeared from nowhere and seized it while the men looked on. They chased the fox, but it got away with its prize.

ON 29 DECEMBER 1805 a man bet that he would run from a house near Swansea Quay to the Angel Inn at Greenhill and back again, a distance of over a mile, before his friend could eat a penny loaf. He ran there and back before his friend had finished the bread.

JOHN MEREDITH LIVED in a cottage at Llanvase, Brecon-shire. In 1781 he put a small eel into a well in his garden. The well was 9 feet deep and 3 feet in diameter and seldom contained more than 2 feet of water – except when the nearby River Usk was swollen by flooding. Then the well filled completely. When this occurred in 1812, the eel appeared on the surface and was caught in a pail by the then tenant Margaret Price. The eel had thrived in the well. It was as thick as her arm and coiled around the pail from bottom to top. She put the eel back in the well.

ON 13 FEBRUARY 1802, for a wager of a guinea, a Welshman, who was an attendant waterman of the stand of coaches in St Paul's churchyard in London, undertook to run from the gate opposite Ludgate Hill eighteen times around the iron railing in the space of an hour. He did it with five minutes to spare and was 'triumphantly led' off to the Spotted Dog Inn to receive his winnings.

KATHERYN TUDOR (c. 1540–91) of Berain famously accepted two proposals of marriage during the funeral of her first husband, who was John Salusbury of Llewenni, Denbighshire. Following his death, she married Sir Richard Clough, who died six years later. She then married Maurice Wynn of Gwydir, who is said to have proposed to her immediately after her first husband's funeral only to find that Clough had got in first. She also outlived Wynn and went on to take Edward Thelwall of Plas-y-ward as her fourth husband. He survived her.

AT THE MACHYNLLETH races in Montgomeryshire in September 1794, the £50 purse was won by Dr Evans's horse *I'm Quick*, beating Mr Lloyd's *Stop Till I Come*, and Mr Vincent Evan's horse *I'm Done For*.

A NOTE ON page 441 of William Robson's 1852 translation of Joseph Michaud's *History of the Crusades* records:

> There is extant in Latin an account of the journey of Archbishop Baldwin through the country of Wales, entitled *Itinerarium Cambriae*, drawn up by Gerald of Wales (*c.* 1146–*c.* 1223), who accompanied the preacher of the crusade. This journey is curious from the singular prodigies and miracles which are related in it. If this relation may be credited, Archbishop Baldwin neglected no means to induce the people to take the cross; he enrolled one day, says Gerald of Wales, a great number of men who came to him in a state of nudity, their clothes being secreted by their wives and friends, who wished to prevent their going.

THE MONTHLY *DISABILITY NOW* of March 1995 tells how a former miner's deafness was cured when a doctor took a small lump of coal out of his ear. When Wrexham doctor Arik Shaik syringed an 83-year-old's ear a piece of coal dropped out and his hearing returned. The old man had been deaf for twenty years, but was unaware of the cause.

A YOUNG WOMAN in Monmouthshire milking a cow was nearly surrounded by the sudden surge of floodwater on 30 January 1607, which covered a large part of south Wales. She managed to escape and, with difficulty, climb a small hill nearby. It was 8 a.m. the next day before anyone spotted her plight. By this time the water had risen so much that there was only a small part of the hill left above water. There were no boats in the area, so some rescuers tried to reach her by swimming a horse to the hill, but they had to turn back.

Next they tied two wide troughs used to salt bacon together with rope and poles to make a double-hulled canoe. Two men got in and propelled the strange craft over to the poor girl, using long poles. They managed to rescue the young woman, who was freezing cold, hungry and terrified by the experience. She had shared her small island with dogs, cats, moles, foxes, hares, rabbits, and even mice and rats, which all had climbed the hill to escape the flood. The girl had great trouble keeping the animals from hurting her or creeping on or around her. During the entire time she noted that natural enemies had not once preyed on each other.

ONE SHORT-SIGHTED HUNTER out grouse shooting in Wales with friends in 1806 is said to have killed a goat instead of a bird.

AFTER DRINKING SOME water from a pond in April 1808, a valuable mare belonging to Samuel Podmore of Hawarden, Flintshire, became unable to swallow anything. She swelled up and lived for a couple of days in agony before dying. The horse was autopsied to discover the cause of death. Nothing out of the normal was discovered in the internal organs, but a large toad was found alive in the poor horse's windpipe. It was presumed that the horse accidentally swallowed the toad while drinking at the pond.

TWO FRENCH OFFICERS were on parole at Brecon in August 1812. One wagered the other that he could not run a quarter of a mile in two minutes in full fishing-dress, with a basket on his back and carrying a rod in his hand. His friend managed to do it with fifty seconds to spare.

TONY SMART OF Newport walked around for ten days in late 1999, unaware that he had a 3-inch nail stuck in his head. A nail gun was accidentally dropped on his head at the factory where he worked. It went off, firing a nail into his skull, but no one realized it. Smart had gone to Casualty at Caerphilly Miners' Hospital where he was treated for a small scalp wound caused by the injury and then released. However, ten days later he collapsed at a Manchester United home match and was taken to Salford's Hope Hospital, where the nail showed up in an X-ray. Amazed surgeons operated to remove the nail and the 38-year-old made a complete recovery.

DAME MORRIS OF Olbaston, near Monmouth, died in April 1805 at the age of ninety. For years she had kept a coffin prepared for her eventual demise. She retained it in her home and used it to store personal belongings and household goods. When the time came for the coffin to be used for its intended purpose, it was found to be full of apples.

AN ILFORD LADY travelling through Wales in 1940 had to spend some hours waiting for a train connection at Brecon. While sheltering from the rain, an umbrella caught in her coat. When she turned around, the woman discovered that the owner was a friend, whose address in Brecon she had forgotten. Going to the friend's home, she met a gentleman from Africa, and during a conversation found that he lived next door to a friend of hers who had emigrated some years previously.

ON 16 MARCH 1839, 7-year-old William Solomans, of Risca, undertook, for a wager of a sovereign, to run from Risca to Newport with the Tredegar coach, and to reach the post office in Newport before it. The boy started at the same time as the coach and kept pace with it until they reached the top of Stow Hill. Then he quickened his pace down the steep descent and outstripped the coach to win the wager, to the 'delight of everyone who witnessed the extraordinary performance'. The distance covered was about seven miles and the boy did it in forty-five minutes, which was remarkable considering his age.

Another remarkable child athlete was 13-year-old Mountjoy Jr, who followed in the footsteps of his famous pedestrian father and astonished the inhabitants of Swansea with his feats. On 8 and 9 March 1844 he walked from Swansea to Neath and back – twice each day – a total of sixty-four miles in both days. After a day's rest, the youth performed some feats at the Cameron Arms bowling green. Over a period of forty-five minutes, the 13-year-old ran half a mile forwards and then walked the same distance backwards. He then walked another quarter of a mile backwards, walked forwards trundling a hoop, then ran and hopped one hundred yards each, before picking up a hundred eggs with his mouth. Finally the boy jumped twenty hurdles that were 2 feet 4½ inches high.

THOMAS WILLIAMS OF Skewen, near Neath, Glamorganshire, owed his life to a dream. For years he crossed the road every day outside his home at exactly the same spot. Then one night he dreamed that while halfway across the road, he was knocked down and killed by a car. The dream was so vivid that the next day Williams crossed the road at a different place. Halfway across he saw a car swerve, mount the pavement, and crash into a lamp-post at the exact spot in his dream. Williams told the story of how his life had been saved when giving evidence in court against the reckless driver in September 1932.

SOMETIME IN 1783 the planks of the bridge at Chepstow, Monmouthshire, had to be removed. Only one was left down for foot passengers. At night the bridge was well lit and a man was stationed to warn of the danger. However, one stormy night the lamps blew out and the guard, presuming no one would travel in such poor weather, abandoned his post and sought shelter. After midnight a traveller knocked at the door of an inn in Chepstow and asked to be admitted. The landlord knew him and let the man in. He was astonished to hear that the man had come on horseback over the bridge, but said nothing. Next day he showed the man the bridge and the single plank his horse had crossed safely. Unnerved by the danger he had escaped, the poor man took to bed and did not recover for some time.

AFTER SHE COMPLAINED of deafness to a doctor, a tooth, carefully wrapped in tissue paper, was removed from 96-year-old Muriel Diceu's ear in September 1979. 'I must have put it on my pillow in 1895 hoping that the fairies would bring me sixpence', the elderly Cardiff woman remarked. 'I have often wondered what became of it and now the mystery is solved.'

A CHILDLESS COUPLE from Abercynon (about fifteen miles north of Cardiff) decided to adopt a child from Belgian refugees in 1915 and travelled to Swansea to do so. They found two orphan children, a brother and sister, whom the authorities did not want to split up, and adopted them. They took them home, fed them and went to put them to bed. The wife discovered a locket hanging around the girl's neck and opened it, hoping it might give some clue to the children's identity. Inside was a photograph which she recognized as that of her sister, who had gone to Belgium as a governess years before, settled down and married. It now appeared she was the mother of the little refugees. The Abercynon woman had unknowingly adopted her own parentless nephew and niece!

A TOMBSTONE IN a churchyard at Penhow, Monmouthshire, is said to bear the following epitaph on a molecatcher:

Here lies William Tandy,
He was very handy,
To catch a mole,
In every hole,
At last the mole caught Tandy.

A RIVER PILOT and a waggoner from Chester fought a duel in a field near Connah's Quay, Flintshire, in March 1811. Having quarrelled over a woman, they decided to settle the matter by trial of arms. They went to a ship to get a brace of pistols, but could not find any. Instead, they made do with two large blunderbusses and loaded them with slugs. With their seconds and around twenty spectators, they met at the agreed place. After pulling off their coats and waistcoats, each tied a handkerchief round his body and defiantly tossed away his hat in bravado. After walking twelve yards apart, they both turned and fired when signalled to do so. Astonishingly, their injuries were slight. One was injured in the nose, the other in the ear.

IN 1907, WILLIAM Porter of 28 Cross Street, Holyhead, Anglesey, sent a photograph to the *Strand Magazine* of himself dressed in an unusual suit of clothes decorated with used tram tickets and stamps. Porter's hat, coat and waist-coat were covered entirely with tickets of various colours and prices. His trousers were completely coated with penny postage stamps. Altogether his odd costume was adorned with 2,544 tickets and stamps.

In 1924 a coastguard stationed at Penbryn, Cardiganshire, found a seagull with a broken wing. He cared for it for some weeks until it recovered, then released it. The next morning at breakfast there was a fluttering of wings at the window. The seagull had returned for a meal. Once fed, it flew off again, but it returned once more at dinner time. For the next twelve years it called twice a day to share the coast-guard's breakfast and dinner.

Newspapers in February 1808 reported that 'an honest farmer' from Ffestiniog, Merionethshire, had died at the age of 105. He had been married three times. He had thirty-three children by his first wife, ten by his second, and four by his third. Additionally, two other women bore him seven children between them. His youngest son was eighty-one years older than the youngest and no less than 800 descendants attended the farmer's funeral.

It used to be a common belief that it was illegal to sell a wife in the marketplace if the husband placed a halter around her neck. However, this practice had no basis in law. In April 1815, 79-year-old pauper, William Jones, who had only been married for three weeks, sold his wife for three halfpence in the marketplace at Llanrwst, Denbighshire.

In a letter to *The Times* of London dated 14 February 1884, William Taylor from Blaendyffryn, Llandysul, Cardiganshire, wrote:

> On Monday morning, during a heavy snowstorm, a huge ball of fire, nearly as large as a barrel, fell within twenty yards of my residence, and when within a few feet of the ground exploded with terrific force. It wrecked every window on that side into 10,000 pieces, mostly thick plate glass. I was sitting with my family at breakfast, and at the moment looking out of the window, so saw everything perfectly. It appeared as though fire was raining from above all round. Another fell 200 yards off, burying into the ground 3ft., and destroying my water supply. Another fell at a farm a quarter of a mile off, destroying a building, and stripping an immense tree from top to bottom, and threw down four horses at work. It was the most appalling sight a human being could witness, and I could only imagine the end of all things had arrived.

On 27 June 1891 a Swansea fisherman hooked a swallow while out trout fishing at Pantyffynon, Carmarthenshire.

In Wales in 2008 a veteran motorist ended seventy-six years of trouble-free driving by smashing his Ford Fiesta into two Porsches, Dukes of Hazard style. Jack Higgs, aged ninety-three, was parking next to a Porsche showroom in Penarth, near Cardiff, when his foot slipped, causing his car to shoot backwards. First he hit a red Carrera 2, which then acted as a ramp, flipping his car on to the silver Porsche 911 parked alongside. Shocked staff discovered the pensioner hanging upside down by his seatbelt in his 13-year-old car. The incident caused £60,000 worth of damage.

Dave Coombs, a dealer at the showroom, said: 'It was amazing. We could hardly believe our eyes at the damage. There was glass and bits of broken metal everywhere, but Jack is such a gentleman, he asked for a sweeping brush to help clear them up. I'm not too concerned about the cars – what matters is that Jack survived, which is incredible considering his great age.'

IT APPEARS THAT, in times past, one could slander anyone without fear of libel laws:

CAUTION. — Whereas a woman, passing by the name of Elizabeth Watkins, who hires herself occasionally as cook, and in which capacity she lived in the advertiser's service for four months, has proved herself to be of notoriously bad character. This is to caution heads of families against employing her, as she is totally unworthy of trust. She is of middle age, thin, and slight stature, with sunken and squinting eyes; altogether a very forbidding countenance.
COLTHURST BATEMAN.
Bertholey House, Monmouthshire,
April 25th, 1833

THE FOLLOWING HANDBILL was issued by Robert Edwards of Pen-y-bont, near Dolgellau, Merionethshire, early in the nineteenth century:

Robert Edwards

Second son of the celebrated Tanner, William Edwards, ap Thomas, ap William, ap David, ap Owen, great, great, great grandson of Cadwgan, a lineal descendant of Bleddyn ap Cyfnfyn Prince of Powys. Since his nativity the sun hath eighty times travelled to its summer solstice. (He will be 80 in March, 1803.) Fifty years was the Host of the Hen and Chickens Alehouse, Pen-y-bont, twenty of which he was Apparitor to the late Right Reverend Father in God John Lord Bishop of Bangor and his Predecessor: by Chance made Glover, by Genius, a Fly-dresser and Angler. Is now by Divine assistance, Conductor to and over the Cadair Idris, to the stupendous Cataracts of Cain and Mowddach, and to the enchanting Cascades of Dol-y-melynllyn, with all its beautifully and romantic scenery; Guide general and grand Expounder of all the Curiosities of North Wales; Knight of the most eccentric (and perhaps happy) order of Hair brained Inexplicables.

WILLIAM LEWIS OF Llanddyfnan, Anglesey, was an eccentric glutton, known by the nickname of 'King of Spain'. When he died on 13 December 1797 he weighed an incredible 40 stone. He died in his parlour, which was lucky because it would have been impossible to carry his corpse down the stairs. A crane had to lift his body onto a carriage for burial. At the graveyard the crane was used to let Lewis down into the grave.

Lewis used to read a couple of chapters of the Bible in the morning and drink copious amounts of ale every night. It was estimated that over his lifetime he must have drunk a sufficient amount of ale to float a 74-gun warship.

IN FEBRUARY 1884 the former manager of a Rhondda colliery told a journalist about an instance of fore-boding that saved his life. Sitting one morning with three colleagues in the lodge room at the bottom of a shaft, he suddenly had the urge to ascend at once, fearing that some-thing bad was going to happen. He told his friends, but they ignored him and refused to go. While talking, a drop of water from the wall put out one man's lamp, and he had to take a lift to the surface.

When he returned, the manager's sense of foreboding made him urge his friends to get out of the shaft. Again, a drop of water fell and put out a lamp. Alarmed by this, the others agreed to leave the pit and they jumped into the lift. No sooner had they reached the surface than a terrible explosion occurred beneath them, destroying the mine shaft they had just left. It took months to clear it.

IN 1828 A favourite pony mare belonging to Mr Field Evans of Henfaes, Montgomeryshire, had a colt foal and both grazed in a field next to the River Severn. One day the mare appeared in front of Mr Evans's house and whinnied to attract attention. When someone went out, she galloped off. Evans followed and found all the gates from the house to the field forced open. When he reached the field, the mare was found looking into the river, over the spot where the colt was found drowned.

WHEN LEWIS OWEN was sentenced to death at Caernarvon Assizes in 1822 for shooting an excise officer during a robbery near Llanrwst, Denbighshire, the townspeople petitioned in vain for a reprieve. No carpenter could be found from the town to build the gallows. After some difficulty the job was undertaken and completed in Pwllheli. It was brought to the place of execution in the dead of night but no one would erected it, so the sheriff and his servants did the work.

A cart was needed to convey the condemned man to the gallows. The sheriff wanted to use one belonging to a carrier, but the owner, a woman, pleaded with him not to take a cart because no one would hire her to carry goods afterwards. They took pity on the woman and, instead, used one belonging to an innkeeper, removed his name from it and painted it black. When the execution was over, no one could be found to take down the gallows. The townspeople were said to be horrified by the man's execution. The hangman, returning to Chester by mail coach, was recognized by his fellow passengers. They refused to let the coach proceed until the coachman had ejected him.

RICHARD WILLIAMS OF the parish of Heneglwys, Anglesey, died in 1809 aged 103. He had been blind for six years, but his sight was restored a short while before his death. He also cut four new teeth.

A WELSH BUTCHER issued an apology in the *Cambrian* newspaper of 17 June 1808 to a gentleman to whom he had sold a loin of veal in Swansea market. Under the kidney fat of the meat, he had stuffed an amount of rags and paper so cunningly that the meat was cooked before the trick was discovered.

PETER CROKE WAS playing a round of golf with his friend John Maher at Southerndown Golf Club near Porthcawl in Glamorganshire on 1 June 1995 when an unusual freak accident occurred. Croke's drive on the seventeenth tee went up a sheep's rear end and the ball was then carried by the animal 30 yards closer to the green.

ENTERPRISING SWANSEA UNIVERSITY students hoaxed the people of Neath in November 1928 while raising money for Swansea Hospital. When sandwich men paraded around the town announcing the surprise visit of Aimee McPherson (a famous celebrity evangelist of the day) for the afternoon, a large crowd gathered at the railway station to welcome her. 'Aimee' wore a luminous black dress and a vivid red wig. She cried, 'Glory, glory. We have come to preach on behalf of the Swansea Hospital. We want you to give until it hurts. You shall be robbed right and left.' A large sum was raised for the hospital by the enterprising hoaxers.

IN MAY 1822 Daniel Evans of Llangwathan, Pembrokeshire, decided to buy a coffin to have it ready to bury his seriously ill wife, who was not expected to live long. After buying one in Fishguard, he got drunk before returning home. He died the next morning and was buried in the coffin he had bought for his beloved wife. She, on the other hand, made a full recovery.

AT FLINT ASSIZES in 1818, a rogue was convicted of obtaining money under false pretences by swindling a deluded farmer of fifteen shillings. He convinced the poor man that his name had been put into a certain well, and that, while it remained there, he would not prosper. The swindler undertook to get the man's name out of this unlucky well for fifteen shillings, and prayers, invocations and psalms were resorted to for the purpose. He was sentenced to a year's imprisonment, as a warning to all others, for conning the ignorant and superstitious country people of the locality.

WELSHMAN BRIAN EVANS had to change his name to Evangelo Brioni when he was promoted to the position of banqueting manager of the famous Savoy Hotel in London in 1961, because the Savoy board of directors insisted that their banqueting manager should have an Italian name.

IN AUGUST 1979 David Jeremy, a carpenter from Merthyr Tydfil, was fined £18 for trying to obtain a passport in the name of Nassa Ocovish. He said:

I fell in love with Miss Jane Plum at first sight. When she told me that she was interested in foreigners, I told her that I was the son of a Puerto Rican uranium miner called Nassa Ocovish – a name that just came into my mind. For two years she has known me as Nassa. Whenever we went out, I had to pick places where I was unknown. But there were always people around who used to shout "Hullo, Dave" and things like that. Finally I decided to get a document that would prove who I was, but it was my undoing.

IN NOVEMBER 1911, a Monmouth girl sleepwalked barefooted in her nightdress for four miles before being awakened by the shock of stumbling and falling. She lived in a house a mile outside the town and got out of bed in the night and unlocked the house door without awakening anyone else in the house. She picked her way in darkness through an outhouse used to store firewood and coal and walked through Monmouth in the direction of her parents' home seven miles away, in the Forest of Dean. When she stumbled and fell, the girl awoke, then continued on to her parents' home, arriving there at three o'clock in the morning.

SAM LEDWARD FROM Gwernaffield, Flintshire, celebrated his birthday in November 2012 – seventy-six years after he was declared dead. Ledward was just thirty when he crashed his motorbike in 1936 and went into a deep coma. Doctors thought he was dead and ordered his body be taken to the mortuary. On the way a hospital porter noticed his 'corpse' move and returned him to the ward. Ledward came to five days later and made a full recovery.

In April 1913 three men from Llandudno, Caernarvonshire, went out to sea in a small boat to fish. Suddenly dense fog descended and they lost their bearings. They rowed for hours but could not see any sign of land. The exhausted men were about to anchor and rest when they spotted a flock of seagulls. They reasoned that the birds were making for either the Great Orme or Little Orme headlands to roost and they followed them to land.

A flutter of excitement ran through the bird-watching community when a new type of bird was spotted near Swansea in October 2008. It had a yellow breast of a bright hue never before seen in nature. More than sixty birdwatchers reported sightings of this unusual new species of oystercatcher before the truth emerged. Scientists had actually marked 150 oystercatchers with yellow dye as part of a research project into flight patterns and had released the birds off the South Wales coastline.

In June 2006 a hamster survived being put through a recycling plant. Somehow, the unfortunate animal came to be in a white goods skip that was delivered to a recycling plant in Sandycroft, Flintshire. There it was tipped onto a conveyor belt, along with hundreds of tons of waste. The tiny rodent survived going through a huge industrial shredder, which could rip a cooker or washing machine to pieces in seconds. Then it was tipped into a revolving drum, before being shaken up on vibrating grids used to separate smaller pieces of scrap.

Workers at the plant were amazed when the quivering and unkempt hamster emerged from the machinery looking a little dazed and suffering from nothing other than a sore foot. Machine operator Craig Bull found the hamster sitting among a pile of shredded waste and took him home to be looked after by his 10-year-old son, Craig. It seems the lucky hamster was small enough to pass through the 6-inch gaps between the shredder blades, and yet big enough to ride along the grids without falling through.

VARIOUS NEWSPAPERS OF April 1772 recorded the death of the 'mighty man of Usk' in Monmouthshire. Philip Mason was an enormous man. 'He measured 11 inches round the wrist; at his arm, near the shoulder, 21 inches; round the breast, 5 feet; body, 6 feet 1 inch; thigh, 3 feet 1 inch; calf of the leg, 2 feet 1 inch; and small calf, 1 foot 7 inches.' Despite his great bulk Mason was a very active man.

He was buried in the graveyard of the Priory Church of St Mary where his gravestone can still be seen. According to the inscription, Mason died aged fifty-one, weighing 554 lb, or just under 40 stone.

THE DEATH, FROM a tragic accident, of David David of Llantwit Major in the Vale of Glamorgan in August 1878, was a sad end to a remarkable life. At the age of sixteen David had joined the Royal Navy and served with distinction for many years. He was also a friend of the Rajah of

Sarawak. He fought in several 'severe battles' with pirates – particularly against the notorious Dyaks of Borneo. Once David was pinned by a cutlass to the mast, and left there while the vessel was taken and retaken. The wound festered and David became seriously ill. He did recover, however, and returned home to Llantwit Major with a large sum of prize money he had won.

THE FOLLOWING ARE among the very curious items of a Welsh female doctor's bill for the cure of a sore leg, and for payment of which the patient was summoned before the court of requests at Shrewsbury.

	s.	d.
❖ For lancing and scalin the poune	10	0
❖ For pills aurea, giltet with golt	7	6
❖ For trams and cordivolls for hur an company	7	6
❖ For lodgen an attendance upon hur	2	6
❖ For runnin away an hindrin me to hav time to cur her to perfection	2	6
❖ For envy, hatred, an mallis, an for uttring several false storees on me an my hous	10	6
❖ For prakin the class in the class windos with her horsis nose	1	0

ELIZABETH RANDLES (1799–1829) of Wrexham was a child prodigy. Her father Edward was a church organist and a very talented harpist. This was all the more remarkable since he was blind. With such a musical heritage, it is little wonder his daughter was also gifted. Elizabeth first performed for the public at the age of two, playing '*Ar Hyd y Nos*,' and 'The Downfall of Paris', on the piano at the Wrexham Theatre. Before she was four, Elizabeth performed a concert for King George III and Queen Charlotte at court and the royal couple were highly impressed.

With the patronage of royalty and high society, a large sum of money was raised for the musical wonder. It is said that, by the time she reached the age of six, this extraordinary child could play 'the most complicated music and sing anything laid before her at first sight'. As she grew up, Elizabeth became a first-rate performer on both the harp and the piano. As a child she was great friends with Caroline, Princess of Wales. On one occasion the two were overheard chatting.

'Do you know, Bessie, that my grandfather is King of England, and that my father is Prince of Wales?'

'Well,' replied the little Welsh lassie, 'and my father is organist of Wrexham.'

AN EXPLOSION OCCURRED at Welshpool, Montgomeryshire, about 4 a.m. on 23 December 1813 when the warehouse of Mr Griffiths, a grocer, caught fire and five barrels of gunpowder exploded, blowing the warehouse and its contents in every direction. An adjoining house was damaged and the windows of many neighbouring dwellings were shattered. The explosion caused the landlady of the town's Britannia Inn to die of fright.

THE *DAILY TELEGRAPH* of 13 July 1982 carried a sad tale. A village teacher in South Glamorgan had fired his starting pistol to demonstrate what pupils would hear on sports day, and the class's pet hamster died of a heart attack.

LOCATED IMMEDIATELY INSIDE the gates of the churchyard of St Aelhaiarn's in Guilsfield Church in Montgomeryshire is a table tomb with a curious weathered inscription:

Here lyeth ye body of Richard Jones
of Moysgwin, gent,
who was interred December ye 10th 1707
aged 90.
Under this yew tree,
Buried would hee be,
For his father and hee,
Planted this yew tree.

The tomb is overshadowed by the yew tree referred to in the epitaph.

THE *GENTLEMAN'S MAGAZINE* records a terrible tragedy that befell an unfortunate family on 17 December 1814 at their home at Moughtre, near Newtown, Montgomeryshire. Their cottage was built under a steep bank. Heavy rains had loosened the earth and a 'torrent of mud' overwhelmed the house with the two parents and five small children inside. Two of the younger children died.

The husband was driven outside the cottage by the mudslide and 'there fixed in the surrounding ruin, a distressed spectator of the sufferings of his family, without being able to stir to their assistance'. His wife was forced onto the fire in the grate and her legs were badly burnt. They remained in their helpless positions for two hours until their neighbours were able to free them.

WILLIAM BEEVAN FROM Llanthomas, Hay, Breconshire, died at the age of 105 in September 1879 and was buried in Talgarth churchyard with all due ceremony. He was never known to have received medical aid of any kind. When he was a hundred, his friends thought it prudent to summon a doctor to treat a minor ailment. Beevan got wind of this unwelcome visitor and hid himself in a closet until the unwanted medic had left.

WHILE PLAYING IN the *News Chronicle*'s £1,000 tournament at Brighton in August 1939, Welsh golfer E.S. Jones hit a ball into a spectator's shirt pocket. The spectator offered to allow Jones to play from his pocket, but the golfer declined. The spectator dropped the ball and Jones played it without being penalized, but, according to the rules, Jones should himself have dropped the ball.

A 'LADY AERONAUT' named Miss O'Neill had a close shave at Pontypool on 7 June 1906. She had planned to ascend to a high altitude in a balloon, then release a parachute and float gently back to earth. Just as the balloon was released, Miss O'Neill got a foot caught in the rope-work of the balloon platform. Before she could free herself, the balloon soared, leaving the young woman hanging head downwards by her feet.

Despite her perilous situation, the woman's courage did not desert her. Grabbing a loose rope, she pulled herself up with great difficulty and freed her leg. Once safely on the platform, she yanked the rope that detached the parachute and bravely held on while she descended safely to earth, none the worse for her ordeal.

RAY ACKROYD AND his wife Mary adopted two orphaned brothers, Rod and Shankill Davis, when his regiment was stationed in Wales in 1942. By June 1991 Ackroyd was eighty-seven years old and blind. He had lost touch with the brothers thirty years earlier, but yearned to meet them again. He saved his pension money and hired a taxi to drive him from his home in Winston, Co. Durham, 250 miles to Aberaeron, Cardiganshire, where he had last heard of them living. On arriving at the town, the taxi driver flagged down an approaching car and asked the driver if he knew Rod Davis. The man replied: 'I'm Rod Davis'. Shortly after-wards the delighted war veteran was reunited with Shankill as well.

NINETEEN MINERS WERE working in the Pentre'r-fron Colliery, near Wrexham, on 27 September 1819 when a tragic accident occurred. The mine had been nearly worked out to the boundary line and the owners had been careful to survey the workings to make sure the miners kept clear of adjoining pits. Despite these precautions, one of the miners struck his pick through the coal into some old workings of another pit and immediately a huge torrent of water burst into the mine.

Sixteen of the men escaped, but the three others were cut off from safety. The mine filled with water and it was nine days before it could be pumped out enough to search for the missing men. The bodies of two men were found on the first day of the search. Twelve days after the accident the remaining miner, John Evans, was found alive. During his entombment, he had only water to drink. What air there was noxious and foul. It caused swellings on his body, especially on his tongue. The man's only protection came from covering his face with his flannel shirt. A few years earlier, this man had been in a mine explosion, in which many lives had been lost while he had escaped unhurt.

THE BEEHIVE INN is a popular roadside inn at Manafon, Montgomeryshire. In the nineteenth century it was famous for the sign over its door with the quaint rhyming inscription:

> within this hive are all alive,
> good liquor makes us funny;
> if you are dry, come in and try,
> the flavour of our honey.

Perhaps this inscription still exists?

IN MAY 1989 the crew of the yacht *Crynogwyn* rescued a dog they found swimming two miles out to sea off St David's Head, Pembrokeshire.

NEIL SIMONS ROBBED a Cardiff petrol station on 28 October 2010 wearing a mask he had bought in the shop three days earlier. He had been the only person to buy the mask. In January 2011 Simons was jailed for the crime.

IN NOVEMBER 1991 two policemen in Newport reported seeing a young woman in a window brandishing a weapon. Armed police surrounded the flat for three hours and police vans blocked off all approaching roads. Eventually, two terrified teenagers emerged, shouting 'Hold your fire!' What the policemen had seen was a 13-year-old girl holding a television remote control.

WHILE WALKING ON the shoreline at Pwllheli, Caernavonshire, in November 1991, a man saw part of a human body in an advanced state of decomposition. He alerted the police. They took the denim-clad corpse to Home Office pathologist Donald Wayte in Bangor. When Wayte cut into it, he discovered it was only a latex mannequin.

MR C. SMART of Chepstow, Monmouthshire, was leading a lively horse over the Chepstow bridge in July 1801 when an accident occurred. The bridge was a wooden one and under repair at the time. Since there were gaps in parts of the flooring, Smart blindfolded the horse to take it across the bridge. As they made their way across, the horse became restless and could not be controlled. It broke away from Smart, turned slightly, and got between two rafters, where the timbers had not been replaced. After being jammed in, and suspended for a few seconds, the horse slipped down and dropped into the river some fifty feet below. Despite the height of the fall, the horse was uninjured, except for having a little hair rubbed off its sides. It swam to the riverbank and sprightly got ashore.

WHEN VILLAGERS IN Moelfre, Anglesey, heard meowing from inside a recycling bin in November 2011, they assumed it was a local pregnant cat which had gone missing some days earlier. They tried to open the container but were unable to do so. Firefighters and the RSPCA were then called, but they too could not prise open the bin. It was transported to a specialist engineering firm eighteen miles away and workers used steel saws to cut off the top. A careful search was made of all the bags, but no cat was found. Inside a bag of toys, one of the searchers picked out a toy cat and wondered if it had been the source of the noise. As he held it, it went off meowing, leaving the rescuers embarrassed by the discovery of the battery-powered toy cat.

THE ONLY TWO men in Britain called Geraint Woolford ended up in adjacent beds in Abergele Hospital, North Wales, in November 2009. The men had never met and were not related. However, they were both retired from the same police force. Also 77-year-old Geraint Woolford, who was in hospital for a hip replacement, was a past president of the Conservative club in his home town of Llandudno. His 58-year-old namesake was a vice-chairman of the Conservative club in Ruthin.

In July 1922 Sidney Peters from Mold, Flintshire, was attacked by a stray bull, but was saved by his own herd of cows. After finding the animal on his land, Peters had tried to remove it, but the bull charged him and tossed him three times. Peters' cows came to his aid. As he lay injured on the ground, they surrounded the farmer and guarded him until help arrived.

When a wedding took place at Porthcawl, Glamorganshire, on 1 January 1927, it was quite an aviary! The bride's surname was Pheasant, the groom's was Partridge, the officiating clergyman was Reverend Woodcock and one of the bridesmaids was a Miss Dove.

While a farmer was moving a flock of sheep along the road near Bala, Merionethshire, in March 1924, a ram broke away and leapt from the Glyn viaduct, which was 150 feet high. The farmer rushed to the spot, expecting to find the animal's dead body. Instead, he saw the ram was travelling at full speed to rejoin the flock. It had landed on soft ground, picked itself up and was none the worse for the experience.

Cardiff steeplejack Albert Melia was working some ninety feet above the ground on a chimney at Newport in October 1926 when he slipped off the platform. He fell some thirty feet, but managed to grab a rope which was hanging from the top. The rope checked his fall and he slid to the ground. He was unhurt except for the rope burns on his hands.

ON 25 JULY 1948, 20-month-old Susan Murray was sleeping in her pram at Prestatyn, Denbighshire, when it suddenly rolled downhill into the path of a bus full of people. The driver tried in vain to avoid the pram but failed and it lodged under the radiator stop. When passengers released the battered pram, they found the baby fast asleep. She had escaped without a scratch.

IN APRIL 1928 Mr and Mrs Harry Jenkins and their ten children were asleep at their home 19 Dyffryn Road, Alltwen, Pontardawe, in the Swansea Valley, when a boulder rolled down the mountainside above them and crashed into the house. It smashed into a bedroom at the back of the house where three children were asleep. Amazingly, the children did not wake, although the family's neighbours were woken by the noise. The boulder continued through the house, demolishing everything in its path in the kitchen, scullery and bathroom. Luckily, no one was hurt.

LLADD DAFAD DDALL, is a Welsh palindrome meaning 'Kill a blind ewe'.

A DUCK STARTED a gold rush in the Vale of Clwyd, Denbighshire, in April 1932 when thirteen pieces of gold was found in the duck's gizzard after it was killed. Prospectors quickly flocked to pan the streams for gold in the area where the duck was reared.

A STRANGE MEETING took place in Australia in August 1945. Lieutenant Gwyn Roberts of Llandrindod Wells, Radnorshire, stopped a stranger on Sydney's Castlereagh Street and asked for directions to his destination. The stranger immediately knew by his accent that Roberts was Welsh, as was he. They soon discovered that they knew the same places and people in Wales. Their mothers were sisters, and so they were cousins. The stranger was Redvers Buller Mason, who had emigrated to Australia twenty years earlier. The men quickly retired to the nearest bar to celebrate their good fortune.

A SMALL WHITE mongrel dog saved the life of 9-year-old Valerie Parry, when she was attacked by a bull terrier at her home near Merthyr Tydfil, Glamorganshire, on 2 November 1948. The mongrel sprang at the terrier and a fierce fight began. While the dogs fought, Valerie's mother rescued her and took her to hospital, where she needed twenty-five stitches in her face. The terrier was later destroyed, while the mongrel was nowhere to be seen.

MR T.J. OSBORNE of Old Market Street, Neath, had a heart-stopping adventure at the Bridge Hotel in Llandrindod Wells in Radnorshire on 30 June 1889. At 3.30 p.m. Osborne was about to leave the hotel to catch a train home, when a full-grown lion jumped in through an open window. Osborne seized a chair and prepared to defend himself, but had the presence of mind to remain calm. At that moment, the animal's keeper and a gang of men with ropes and equipment arrived on the scene to capture the creature. The keeper warned Osborne not to move but to remain quiet. With some difficulty a sack was thrown over the lion's head and the animal was firmly secured with ropes. The lion had escaped from Wombwell's Menagerie, which was halted on a site near the hotel.

A SUPERSTITIOUS MINER in north Wales in July 1903 saved his life by holding true to his beliefs. He was boring under some coal when he was startled by a rat scurrying away. The miner immediately walked away from the spot. A short while later the coal seam collapsed over the place where he had been working.

JOCK WAS A championship-winning sheepdog belonging to Mr G. Pugh of Bedol Farm, Bagillt, Flintshire. In 1954 he won the Welsh sheepdog championship. He was also famous for being the only working sheepdog in Britain or Ireland with a dyed coat. Jock's natural colour was pure white, which not only confused his master, but also the sheep – who followed Jock, thinking he was just another sheep. To get over this difficulty Jock's coat was partially dyed black. Jock had no objection to the change and remained a first-class sheepdog.

IN NOVEMBER 1938 Percy Hayward from Brynmawr, Breconshire, was buried for twenty-seven hours at the bottom of a 20-foot deep shaft until rescuers were able to dig him out. The 36-year-old was scooping coal from a hole so narrow that only one man could stand in it. When the sides collapsed, Hayward was buried up to his waist. His fellow miners worked for hours to release him. At one point they had freed him except for his ankles and feet, when another fall buried him up to his neck. More rescuers were brought in and they worked in relays to dig out the unfortunate man.

MR EVAN JONES of Trimsaran, near Llanelli, Carmarthenshire, was accidentally shot by one of his dogs in November 1923. Jones had gone out shooting on his estate with two dogs. When it began raining, he sought shelter under a tree, placing his gun beneath a hedge. Suddenly the gun was discharged and Jones was wounded in the shoulder. The dogs were playing at the time and it was believed that one of them must have touched the gun's trigger.

IN JANUARY 1879 70-year-old former shoemaker Joseph Mason was prosecuted for failing to support his wife and leaving her dependent on the Aberystwyth union workhouse. Mason had deserted his wife and fled into the mountains miles above the lead mines of Goginan to eke out a hermit's existence. After the workhouse had pressed charges against Mason, a police officer named Jones was given the job of tracking down the elderly man and bringing him to justice.

At Goginan locals directed the officer towards Mason's miserable dwelling. After a great deal of searching, he found it. Although locals had warned him not to approach the angry and unpredictable hermit, the constable was determined to carry out his duty. He opened the door of the hovel and looked in. In the gloomy interior he saw a pile of turf on the floor and a heap of rags that served as the old man's bed. In a corner sat the hermit, glaring at him. Numerous rats were scurrying about. Jones stamped his foot to scare away the vermin, but instead of fleeing, they attacked him, leaping up and biting his trousers. Shocked by this unexpected turn of events, Jones fled.

According to the locals, Mason had 'tamed and trained his strange companions during his sojourn in the mountains, and encouraged them into his house'. Few other details about this strange hermit were recorded, expect that the charges against Joseph Mason were dropped since he was on the verge of starvation himself.

A LEG OF a former sailor was saved from amputation in 2005 by his pet puppy who literally licked the dying limb better. Mitch Bonham, forty-five, of Barry, Glamorgan, was told by a consultant that he would lose his right leg when it began turning black and withering away after a heavy anchor chain fell on his foot and broke a toe when he was serving in the Royal Navy. Bonham developed a condition known as Sudeck's Atrophy, affecting his leg up to the knee.

Hours of physiotherapy failed to stimulate the damaged nerves, and amputation was looking increasingly likely. Then Bonham's Jack Russell puppy, Milo, began licking the toes of the affected right leg, which triggered a cure that medicine had failed to achieve. 'Because he was a puppy at the time, he wouldn't listen to what you wanted him to do, so I just let him keep on licking it', said Bonham. 'He would lick the toe and leg for up to four hours a day. One day, I felt my toe twitch and it was as if my muscles had been reactivated.' Prolonged licking all over the affected area had stimulated nerves and ensured that oxygen reached the leg.

AN AMAZING COINCIDENCE involving Cardigan RNLI took place on 22 June 2010. A lifeboat was launched from Poppit Sands to assist the 13-foot pleasure craft *Glas y Dorlan* (Kingfisher) with two men aboard, which had developed engine trouble off Cardigan Island. As the lifeboat crew towed the afflicted vessel towards shore, they spotted two men in a nearby boat waving frantically. They went to investigate and found the 17-foot boat, also called *Glas y Dorlan*, had broken down. The lifeboat then towed both vessels to shore.

IT IS SAID that Barmouth clergyman Canon Edward Hughes's hair turned white in one night owing to the shock suffered when the new tower of St John's Church in the town collapsed on 11 September 1891.

A PATIENT DISCHARGED himself from a psychiatric unit in Aberystwyth in October 2001 and stole a bus to get home, picking up passengers on the way.

VISITORS TO LLANDUDNO, Caernarvonshire, on 19 August 1904 were treated to the extraordinary sight of a fight between a constable and a monkey. The creature was defending its owner, an Italian, whom the policeman was trying to arrest for begging on the promenade. In court, the Italian claimed that when his monkey took a stroll, people gave it money. The defendant was fined.

IN 1854 A young couple, both aged twenty, married at Llandovery Church in Carmarthenshire. The ceremony passed off without a hitch, but the bride refused to sign the register in the vestry, and despite all efforts to convince her to reconsider, she returned home without offering any explanation to the bridegroom, who went his own way. Fifty years later the groom returned to Llandovery and friends tried to bring the then 90-year-old couple together. The bride explained that the reason for her action was the fear that her small fortune would become her husband's on marriage. 'I loved him,' she said, 'enough to marry him, but I wished to be an independent bride.' She still wore her wedding dress on festive occasions and said she would be buried in it. Before 1883 a woman's property passed to the husband on marriage.

A CAUTIONARY TALE for Good Samaritans was told in a BBC broadcast in May 1969. When a coastguard at Barmouth was told that a woman was screaming in the sea, he rushed in to save her. After bringing her ashore, he applied the standard 'kiss of life'. In the middle of it, the woman slapped him hard on the face.

WHEN JEAN DAWES, a young hairdresser's assistant from Pontypridd, was at Cardiff railway station in July 1930, she was approached by an old lady who explained that she had lost her purse and needed ten shillings for her fare home to Swansea. Jean lent the old woman the money and provided her name and address. The money was returned a few days later, along with a letter of thanks. Fifteen months later Jean was contacted by a firm of Swansea solicitors, who told her that the old lady had died, leaving her £3,000 as a reward for her kindness.

THE RARE *GWYNIAD* is a freshwater whitefish native to Bala Lake, Merionethshire, and is found nowhere else in the world. It developed as a distinct species after it was trapped in the lake at the end of the Ice Age, some 10,000 years ago. Its future survival in the lake is under threat because of deteriorating water quality and the introduction of another fish, the *ruffe*, which is eating the eggs and fry of the *gwyniad*.

WHILE RESEARCHING A book on interesting drunkards in 1901, author Arthur L. Humphreys came across a Cardiff man who had gone out drinking with a label attached to his coat, stating his name and address, asking anyone who found him to bring him home. At the end of the label was the thoughtful note: 'When you prop me against the door, knock, and, for your own sake, don't wait for my wife to thank you!'

HUGH PUGH (1672–1743) was born at Cwmrhwyfor, Tal-y-bont, Cardiganshire. As a boy, he was a noted leaper. One morning, as he was going with his parents to church through Rhiwogo wood, Hugh jumped over his parents' heads without warning. He gave his mother such a fright that she died soon afterwards. Hugh later became a clergyman. In his student days at Oxford he won acclaim as a leaper, a wrestler and a thrower of iron bars.

ARCHDEACON WILLIAM NORTH (d. 1893), rector of Llangoedmor, Cardiganshire, wrote poetry in seven different languages.

DAVID HEWITT (b. 1879), a landscape painter based at Beddgelert, Caernarvonshire, climbed Mount Snowdon over 580 times to sketch and paint, as well as to show novice climbers the beauty of the mountain.

REVEREND JOHN PRICE (1810–95) was the rector of Llanbedr Painscastle, Radnorshire, for nearly four decades. It was a poor parish in a remote area with few parishioners. Reverend Price lived in poverty, first in a hovel then in three old bathing machines which served respectively as a study, bedroom and kitchen. After these burnt down, a brick-and-slate roofed henhouse became his vicarage.

A NEW SPECIES of slug previously unknown to Wales was discovered in 2007. The all-white slug was discovered in a Cardiff garden and in nearby Caerphilly. It was given a partially Welsh name, *Selenochlamys ysbryda* or ghost (*ysbryda*) slug, which is the first time that a Welsh word has been used in a creature's scientific name.

An adult ghost slug is over 7 cm long. It has no eyes and lives underground. Unlike most slugs, it is carnivorous. It eats a diet of mainly earthworms. With its sharp 5 mm teeth, it grips its prey and sucks them in like spaghetti.

The ghost slug belongs to an obscure group of slugs – the *Trigonochlamydidae*. Other slug species in this family are found in Turkey and the Republic of Georgia, but none have been found in Western Europe. Almost certainly an introduced species, its origins and how it arrived in Britain remain a mystery.

DURING THE AUTUMN of 1800 Lee Sugg, a well-known ventriloquist, visited some of the border towns of Wales. Several anecdotes of his tricks are related in newspapers of the day, most likely as advertising puffs. For example, the *Salopian Journal* of 3 September 1800 describes one display of ventriloquism by Sugg at Llanfyllin, Montgomeryshire, which backfired on the performer. He borrowed a mare belonging to a saddler called Davies and rode through the town on market day where a large number of people were gathered. Sugg was not known and went unnoticed until suddenly a voice, seemingly out of the mouth of the mare he was riding, said 'I'll not go any further.'

Sugg answered, 'Come along, come along.'

The mare responded with 'I will be damned if I do.'

'Pray do', said Sugg.

'Not I, by – I will go back', the mare replied.

Sugg now tried to coax her with 'Now, pray go, and I'll give you plenty of corn.'

'Oh! Oh!' said the mare, 'that's another thing' and off she trotted. The newspaper reported that Sugg's performance so alarmed some of the country people, who had intended to see his show, 'that they would never pay two shillings to go to see the devil!'

Mr Davies, whose mare the ventriloquist had ridden, was a man of standing in Llanfyllin and the locality. Over his shop door a sign bore the rhyming inscription:

> Richard Davies he lives here,
> Saddler, Clerk, and Auctioneer.

IN 1882 A French gentleman who had lived in Barmouth for some years died and left an odd request in his will. He wanted to be buried in his garden and ordered that quicklime be thrown in with him. He also requested that his favourite dog be buried with him when it died. Accordingly a hole was blasted in the rocks at the back of his house. The coffin was placed in it, along with a large amount of quicklime. The Church of England Burial Service was read at the grave by the rector, the Reverend John Jones.

AS LATE AS 1835 it seems that some parts of Wales were not free from highwaymen, so wise folk who were travelling alone went armed. The High Sheriff of Montgomeryshire, H.D. Griffith, was going by himself over the Berwyn mountains on 18 February 1835 on his way from his residence at Caer-rhyn in Caernarvonshire to Llechweddgarth Hall, his home in Montgomeryshire, in a pony carriage when two ruffians, armed with bludgeons, jumped out into the road and stopped the carriage. Just as quickly, Griffith whipped out a pair of pistols he had ready for such an event. The men fled.

IN MARCH 1902 S.O. Sanford of Cardiff took a late train to Bristol on business. Sanford and a companion settled down to sleep, but after the train had passed through the Severn Tunnel, Sanford was missed, and could be found nowhere on the train. An engine was telegraphed for at Newport and sent in search of the missing man. He was found in the tunnel, slightly injured. Sanford did not have a clear recollection of how the accident had occurred, but thought he must have opened the carriage door and stepped out. He had been in the Severn Tunnel for two hours in the darkness. During that time several trains had passed him.

PRIVATE W. FAULKNER of the 2nd Welsh Regiment had a close shave on the Western Front in December 1914. In a letter to his mother at the family home in Pontypridd, Glamorgan, he said: 'I had a narrow escape the other day whilst running across the open ground. A bullet went through the pouch of my equipment and through two charges and lodged in the third. I have got the two charges and the German bullet, which I am going to bring home as a curio.'

IN AUGUST 1888 a passer-by was astonished by the sight of a four-legged duck belonging to Mrs Tannant of Tynycoed Cottage, Berriew, Montgomeryshire. This curious freak of nature had four legs, two on each side, one behind the other. The duck was fully grown and all the legs were the same size. While walking, the quadruped duck lifted up its two hind legs, but while swimming it used all four!

PART OF THE Tredegar Arms Hotel at Newport collapsed in June 1924. Five bedrooms, which had been vacated by staff only a few minutes earlier, fell in, and crashed to the ground floor, wrecking several downstairs rooms. Fortunately, no one was injured.

FOR TWO HOURS a 14-year-old black retriever dog defied police efforts to remove its master's bicycle from the scene of an accident. The dog's owner, Bertie Thornton, had fallen and broken a leg at Neath on 29 December 1954. His father had to be brought to the scene to call off the dog, which had been trained to guard the bicycle.

PETER MAINWARING OF Llangeinor, Garw Valley, Glamorgan, owed his life to a bat. The fright it gave him as he lay dying caused him to scream and brought about his recovery. In 1932 the 12-year-old was stricken with a serious illness. The boy was taken to Bridgend Hospital and X-rays revealed something on his lung. Tuberculosis was suspected and Peter was sent to Craig-y-nos sanatorium. Although he received excellent care in the nine weeks he was there, Peter grew worse instead of better. One day his family received a message to go there immediately because Peter was dying. His parents were told to expect the end that night. They took Peter home and made him as comfortable as possible. An extraordinary thing happened during that long night, as his father recalled:

> It was about two o'clock in the morning. I sat in the kitchen, stirring the dying embers of the fire. Mary, my wife, was upstairs, and in the next room lay Peter dying. I heard a scream. I ran into the room. Hurling itself vainly against the half-open window was a tremendous bat trying to escape. It had frightened the dying boy. I let the bat free, and attended to Peter. He coughed badly. With each gasp I thought it would be his last.

The local doctor was called and found a huge molar tooth. Peter's scream and coughs had dislodged the tooth from his lung and he had coughed it up. The point tapered sharply, like the end of a needle. The boy had swallowed the tooth two years earlier, and it had penetrated his lung, causing symptoms like those of tuberculosis. Once Peter coughed up the tooth, his condition improved and he made a full recovery.

An old vestry book from Tregaron parish in Cardiganshire dating from 1636 records that it was the rule of the parish to bury paupers without a coffin, and they were to wear 'their best shoes, their best wearing apparel, and best hat'. The charge for the burial was twopence. If any were buried in a coffin, they also were to don their Sunday best, and the charge for their burial was two shillings and sixpence.

IN APRIL 1924, at the age of eighty-nine, Thomas Griffith of Rhydyclafdy, near Pwllheli, Caernarvonshire, ploughed a field every day for a week. An 87-year-old woman from Aberdare, Glamorgan, ploughed a field behind a pair of oxen for nine hours on 17 June 1817.

THE OLD PARISH books of Llanferres, Flintshire, contain several curious entries. In 1731 the following resolution was made:

> Whereas a certain Drover, Maurice Williams, of the Parish of Llangwm, pretends to have been robbed upon the Highway within the Hundred of Yale of the sum of £102 or thereabouts, and purposes to commence a suit at law against the Hundred for the recovery of the said sum. It is ordered that whatever the Rector, or John Griffiths, shall consent to at the meeting of the several parishes, whether it be to pay our proportion of the said sum, or to stand a trial at law against the Drover, we abide by it, provided on this condition only, that the said parish of Llanferes, in either of the said two cases, do, and shall not pay but its proportion according to the usual rating and assessing of the Quarter tax between the several Parishes of the said Hundred.

A memorandum was later added:

> The Hundred of Yale stood a trial against the above

M. Williams, who thought proper to withdraw his action, and appeared evidently to be a perjured villain. His whole circumstances (as good luck would have it) being well known to certain credible persons. It seems this piece of villainy was his last shift, for soon after he was clapt in prison for debt.

In 1734 Sir John Glynne (1713–77) stood for election as a Member of Parliament for Flint. He spent the huge sum of £25,000 on the campaign, but was still defeated. This did not deter him from trying again. In 1741 he was elected MP for Flintshire and held that position for several years.

According to family legend, Lady Charlotte Williams-Wynn (c. 1754–1830) of Wynnstay House near Ruabon, Denbighshire, was a formidable woman. Once, when travelling from London with her two daughters, a highwayman stopped their carriage and demanded money. Her one concern was that the maid, a good girl who helped to support her own family, should not be robbed of her wages.

After letting herself be stripped of her valuables and money, Lady Williams-Wynn urged her daughters to do likewise. Then she turned to the highwayman, who was clearly not a hardened ruffian, and said 'I suppose, sir, you are too much of a gentleman to think of stealing the hardly earned wages of a poor servant girl.' Her appeal was successful and the highwayman did not rob the girl. Then Lady Williams-Wynn added, 'And now, sir, I trust that you will withdraw that pistol, as I have observed, sir, that your hand shakes very much.'

In 1888 Mr E. Lloyd, a gunmaker of Pontrobert, Montgomeryshire, was sent a gun to be stocked. Taking off the heel-plate, he found a piece of paper enclosed in a small hole. The paper was covered with writing on both sides, and was signed Charles Wm Brooks. This man is better known as Shirley Brooks (1816–74), a famous London-born journalist, novelist and editor of *Punch* magazine in the Victorian era.

As a young man Brooks was apprenticed to his uncle, Charles Sabine, a solicitor in Oswestry, Shropshire. The paper stated that the gun was a present to Brooks from his uncle in the winter of 1830 and a list of several persons who could identify the weapon was on the other side. Brooks also included a short rhyme to make his point clear:

> Steal not this gun for fear of shame,
> For here you see its owner's name;
> And when you die, Old Nick will say –
> Where is that gun you stole away?

When Colonel Edward Pryse from Peithyll, Cardiganshire, died on 29 May 1888 while on his way to fish, news of his death was taken to his niece, Viscountess Parker, by her stepfather, H.C. Fryer. Fryer was surprised at his reception at her home at Montague Square in London, for Viscountess Parker told him, 'Mr Fryer, I know what it is. My uncle is dead. He died on a lane leading from Rhiwarthen to Penwern. I have dreamt four times in four years that this would happen, and the last time was the night before the baby was born. I have tried many times to keep him from going that way.' Afterwards she said she meant the road leading to Penuwch, which is in the same direction, and that she would know the spot.

In Bishop Charles Wordsworth's 1891 book *Annals of My Early Life*, an extract from his diary of 30 November 1829 is given: 'A clergyman doing duty for a friend in Wales was told by an old woman, who filled the situation of clerk, that he must preach in the reading desk, as she had permission to keep her goose in the pulpit.'

When Ralph Griffith became Deputy Sheriff of Flintshire in 1769, one of his duties was to oversee the execution of Edward Edwards for burglary. It was no easy task because Griffith found it impossible to find anyone to be the hangman. He set out the difficulties he faced and the expense undertaken in a petition to the Lords of the Treasury, saying 'That your petitioner was at great difficulty and expense, by himself and his Clerks, and other messengers, and agents he employed, in journeys to Liverpool and Shrewsbury, to hire an Executioner; the convict being a native to Wales, it was almost impossible to procure any of that country to undertake the execution.'

The Deputy Sheriff spent £15 10 shillings on travel and food. He found a Salop native willing to act as executioner and paid him an advance of £5 5 shillings. Another £4 10 shillings was spent hiring two men to accompany this man. Despite this, he gave them the slip on the road and disappeared with the money. A fruitless search was made. After a great deal of trouble and expense, John Babbington, a convict in the same prison as Edwards was persuaded by his wife to execute the condemned man. Babbington's wife was paid £6 6 shillings, as was Babbington himself.

It cost £4 12 shillings to build a gallows. Griffith noted that it was 'a business very difficult to be done in that county'. He also paid out another £7 10 shillings to hire a cart to convey the body, along with the purchase of a coffin and other sundry expenses connected with the burial. In all Griffith spent £49 19 shillings – no small sum of money in those days – and 'humbly hoped' to be reimbursed for his trouble.

IN MAY 1892 Samuel Miller of The Court, Llanmerewig, Montgomeryshire, set a night-line in a small river near his home. During the night it seems that a horse came down to the river to quench its thirst at the spot where the line was laid and somehow got tangled up in the fishing line. As it was struggling to free itself, one of the hooks got caught in its tail. The horse seems to have given up the attempt and wandered back to its grazing. The next morning a pike of about 3 lb weight was found dangling from its tail.

WHILE BERTRAND RUSSELL, born in Trellick, Monmouthshire, was visiting Bejing in the 1930s he became very ill. Japanese reporters in the city constantly tried to see Russell, but were always denied access. They decided he was dead and notified their newspapers of his demise. News of his death spread around the world and it gave Russell a great deal of pleasure to read his obituary notices.

One missionary paper had an obituary of one sentence: 'Missionaries may be pardoned for heaving a sigh of relief at the news of Mr Bertrand Russell's death.' This incident inspired Russell to write his own obituary for *The Times* of London in 1937. He told the newspaper to run it in 1962 – the year he expected to die, but they did not need it until 1970 when he died aged ninety-eight.

ON 23 FEBRUARY 1646, the Parliamentary forces began fortifying Llansilin Church, Denbighshire, to keep the occupants of Chirk Castle in check. When a group of them attacked Ty Mawr in Llansilin, they found the doors well barricaded. The defenders then threw some beehives out amongst the attackers, which routed the enemy.

A WRITER IN the *European Magazine* of March 1782, says:

> On St David's Day my bosom friend, George Fairford, called at my Chambers, and with a boisterous mandate ordered me instantly to set off for Lambeth, to spend the day and the night among the hot-blooded Welshmen. 'We shall have,' says he, 'a world of entertainment for the girls have the prettiest red cheeks, and round faces in the world, and on this day they are as wild and as venturesome as the goats on their mountains.'

ACCORDING TO THE *Notes and Queries* periodical of 1852, an estate in a parish on the coast of Pembrokeshire was exempt from tithes because it gave a cup of ale and an egg to the clergyman for refreshment, whenever the tide compelled him to pass the landowner's house on his way to hold a service in the parish church.

EVAN PRICE OF Llanfyllin, Montgomeryshire, died on 9 January 1820, aged 104 years and 10 months. Until two years before to his death, he was still able to continue his trade as a watch- and clock-maker. To the end of Price's days, his sight was strong enough to allow him to read a newspaper without the aid of glasses.

A MONUMENT TABLET to David Davies lies in St Mary's Church, Llanfair Caereinion, Montgomeryshire. He died at Cheltenham in 1790. Davies's will stipulated that sixpence be given to each poor person who attended his funeral. Some 1,030 such persons were present and each received sixpence.

IN 1838 THIRTY-THREE people fitted inside a hollow elm tree on a farm belonging to one Captain Howell from Cowbridge, Glamorgan. There was still room for three more people if they had been at hand.

IN 1734 A presentment made by a grand jury at Beaumaris, Anglesey, that the judges' lodgings in the town 'ought to be improved' since they were so 'poore and straight that the judge eateth and sleepeth in rooms with earth floors were fowls and other unseemly things do congregate, and noteth his arrival in the town by a flag fixed to a prop which is posted up through the chimney of the house.'

THE NEWSPAPERS OF November 1820 relate the circumstances of the loss of his nose by a man in a fight at Caernarvon. When he came to court to seek damages, no one recognized him as the man who had lost his nose. A skilful Caernarvon surgeon had crafted the man a new one 'out of the integuments of the forehead'. It was said to have looked better than the old nose.

IN OCTOBER 1837 an inquest was held at the Cross Guns, near Llanymynech, Montgomeryshire, on the body of a man who had hanged himself. It was stated that 'to prevent the disgrace of dying in his shoes', he had carefully taken them off.

IN 1714 LLANYCIL Church in Merionethshire was described as being filled with cushions and rushes, for the convenience of the congregation to kneel and sit on. When the rector wanted to remove them, the parishioners refused to comply with his wishes, saying that 'they could not remain comfortable and quiet without them'. The rector was undaunted by their blank refusal and removed some of them, probably in the chancel, where he had more direct control. To his shock, the clergyman discovered that a large number of snakes had sheltered there from the harsh winter. When this was shown to the parishioners, they willingly removed the rushes and cushions.

AN AMATEUR PHOTOGRAPHER was setting up a shot on the cliff at Cemaes Head near Cardigan in September 1994 when he stepped back to improve the photograph and fell around sixty feet down the cliff-face, breaking his leg. Coastguards had to rescue him from a ledge.

THE WONDERFULLY ECLECTIC museum in the town hall of Llanidloes, Montgomeryshire, preserves the stuffed body of a two-headed lamb, which was born locally in 1914.

DURING THE NIGHT of 3 August 1809 the sloop *Recovery*, bound from Newport to Chepstow with a load of coal and iron, broke her cable in gale-force winds, and was driven on shore near the Hook, a short distance from the mouth of the Newport River. Her master, Captain Richards, and a young sailor called Davies, were washed overboard by a huge wave. The captain was drowned, but Davies was washed back on board by another large wave. The sailor quickly climbed the ship's rigging and remained there in 'a very perilous situation' for nearly three hours until the tide went out.

BRITISH POP SINGER Lena Fiagbe turned up for the Radio One Roadshow in Bangor, Caernarvonshire, on the right day in July 1994 and wandered around the town confused, because there was no sign of any such event. Meanwhile in Bangor, County Down, the live radio party was in full swing. What really annoyed Lena was that she had been in Ireland the previous day and had travelled across to north Wales for her next gig. She missed out on the opportunity to sing her smash hit, 'Gotta Get It Right'.

IN JULY 1982 Dr Peter Callaghan from Llanilar, near Aberystwyth, accidentally cast his glasses into the water while fly-fishing on the River Ystwyth. His neighbour William Jones, unaware of the doctor's accident, went fishing in the same river several days later and reeled in the missing glasses.

DURING HIS MARRIAGE ceremony in Conway in August 1978, Harry Vale was surprised when his wife-to-be gave birth to a baby boy in the pew to which he and his best man had carried her. 'It was the first I had heard of it', said Vale, 'but Dora is an assistant nurse, so she knew exactly what to do. When it was all over, we carried on with the wedding as if nothing had happened.'

A SHEEP GOT stuck on the roof of a row of terraced houses in Pontycymmer, Glamorgan, on 11 June 2011. Residents called 999 after the animal was spotted running across roof tiles. Two fire engines were called out to the village and it took forty minutes before the animal was finally caught and brought down, using a large animal rescue appliance. A spokesman for the Bridgend Fire and Rescue Service said the sheep had got onto the roof by climbing up from a garage at the rear of the terrace.

THE DARING RESCUE of a goat from a perilous ledge at Craig Fach Quarry near Barmouth in November 1923 is an astonishing tale. The animal found itself trapped on a dangerous ledge and was unable to escape. Local quarryman Arthur Lloyd volunteered to rescue the goat. A thick board was tied to a heavy rope to give Lloyd a seat and allow him the freedom to use his arms. He was carefully lowered down to the ledge a hundred feet below.

Whether the animal misunderstood its would-be rescuer's intentions or not, it lowered its head and butted Lloyd in the back. This went on for several minutes and Lloyd swung around the cliff face until he was able to swing back in such a way that he got his legs tightly around the neck and head of the goat. He then gave the signal to haul up and he and his captive were pulled to safety.

IN THE NINETEENTH century T.J. Llewelyn Prichard from Builth Wells in Breconshire was a well-known and versatile writer, but he was most notable an account of his artificial wax nose, which was kept in place by his spectacles. He supposedly lost his nose in a fencing match.

A CURIOUS CASE was brought to court in Pontypridd, Glamorgan, in July 1886 when a 103-year-old widow, Elizabeth Hughes from Graig Mountain, was charged with stealing a cheque for £5 14s. It appears she had gone to an insurance agent for her policy, and while she was there the postman placed a letter on the table for the agent. The aged widow seized the letter and left. She was followed home by the police, who found the letter and cheque in her possession. In reply to the magistrates, Mrs Hughes said she was only 102 years old. In her defence the widow claimed she thought she was only taking the policy from the agent's office. The case was withdrawn in consideration of her great age.

IN THE PARISH of Llandrillo-yn-Rhos, near Colwyn Bay, there was a well-known fish-weir made with wooden stakes, enclosing part of the sea at high tide. When the tide receded, the fish were left in the weir. The rector of Llandrillo once had a right to a tithe of all fish caught in it. Every tenth day, the rector was allowed to take all the fish caught in the weir by the two tides.

WHILE CUTTING DOWN a large sycamore in November 1886 on the Duke of Westminster's estate at Halkyn, Flintshire, the men felling the tree struck against something hard. They later discovered a cannonball weighing 10 lb in a cavity in the heart of the tree, which was 6 feet in circumference. The ball must have been in this position for a long time and to have been shot there when the sycamore was young, because there were no markings on the bark to show that the tree had been damaged. The sycamore was sited not far from the old ramparts of Foel Gaer.

A TWO-HEADED TROUT was caught in the River Cleddau in Pembrokeshire in May 1805.

LEE HADWIN OF Henllan, near Denbigh, is a talented artist while asleep! The 36-year-old has been a sleepwalker from an early age. When asleep, he produces amazing pictures on various surfaces around his house. Hadwin never has any recollection of doing drawings and cannot recreate these works of art when he is awake.

As LATE AS 1800 a peculiar funeral custom existed in Defynnock parish, Breconshire. The parish clerk or sexton claimed and received mortuaries on the interment of every person, except paupers, and the residents of Trecastle (who paid fourpence instead). This claim was recognized by the clergyman and parishioners and confirmed by the ecclesiastical court. These mortuaries consisted of the best wig, hat, cravat, gloves, belt, breeches, shoes and stockings of the deceased, if a male. If a widow or wife, the best hood, cap, ribbon, handkerchief, gloves, shoes and stockings were to be given.

ARCHDEACON DAVIES OF Breconshire actively policed his diocese and little escaped his notice. Early one morning, he unexpectedly visited a church, which he knew was in a dilapidated state. He called at the parish clerk's house for the keys. The man, not wanting the archdeacon to see the church, hid the keys in his pocket and said he could not find them. Jokingly, the archdeacon called out to his dog: 'Hi! Collier, keys.' Whether the dog heard the keys jingling in the man's pocket or not, he went up to the clerk, put his nose into his tailcoat pocket and drew out the keys, much to the clerk's discomfort.

WELSH HISTORY IS replete with curious characters performing unusual feats. For a considerable wager, two Neath gentleman ran a foot race against each other on 19 April 1804. One man was to run 100 yards carrying a person weighing 11 stone 2 lb, while his opponent had to run 200 yards carrying nobody. Despite the extra weight, the first man won the race easily.

A CURIOUS CUSTOM known as douching was carried out at Towyn, Merionethshire, until the 1830s. On May Day young men of the town lay in wait with pails of water and, when a young woman was spotted on the street, the water was thrown over her. On 12 May, old May Day, the women returned the compliment, and douched the men. The custom ended in the 1830s after a delicate girl driving into Towyn from Dolgellau with a friend had a pailful of water thrown over her. The shock was so great that she died. The custom stopped after this tragedy.

ON 17 OCTOBER 2010 the organizers of the Cardiff half-marathon blundered. The original route had to be changed for health and safety reasons because of building work on a section of the route, but no one thought to check the length of the adjusted course before the race went ahead. Instead of running 13.1 miles, the 15,000 amateur athletes ended up running 12.98 miles. The mistake

became known when athletes using satellite navigation devices to measure the distance and times discovered the error and reported it. The organizers subsequently issued an apology to the runners.

THE CASE OF 17-year-old Mary Morgan was a particularly sad one and is still remembered – in part – because she has two headstones in the churchyard of St Andrew's in Presteigne, Radnorshire. She was hanged on 13 April 1805 for stabbing to death her newborn baby. Mary was the last woman to be publicly executed in Wales. One headstone has a lengthy and sanctimonious inscription telling of Mary's 'sin and shame', while the second stone nearby simply says, 'He that is without sin among you, let him first cast a stone at her.'

ON 26 JULY 1814 the brig *Eliza* of Cardigan, commanded by W. Davies, the brig *Mary* of Waterford and the brig *Irish Miner* of Cardigan were taken off the coast of Ireland by the armed American privateer, the *Whig*, commanded by Captain Clark. The privateers took the *Mary*'s crew prisoner and set fire to the ship after plundering it. When Captain Clark went on board the *Eliza* and saw that its cargo was of no use to him, he was about to give the order to burn the ship when he spotted a little box in the cabin with a hole in the top and asked what it was. Captain Davies explained that he and every member of the crew put a penny in the box each week to save money, for the purpose of sending out missionaries to preach the Gospel to the heathen. When Captain Clark heard this he said, 'Captain, we Americans

are not at war with you, nor with the likes of you, but with your cursed Government we are at war. As the cargo belongs to your Government, I will utterly destroy it, but neither you nor your vessel will I by any means hurt.'

The Americans threw 637 sacks of corn overboard and destroyed the rest by pouring seawater over them. When Captain Clark learned that the third ship, the *Irish Miner*, belonged in part to Davies, he spared her cargo altogether. So the missionary box saved two ships and one cargo. Before leaving, the Captain made Davies promise to come and see him if he was captured and give him £50 for each of the two ships he had spared. Davies willingly made the promise, but whether he was ever called on to keep his word is not recorded. The reward given to him by the under-writers at Lloyd's certainly would not have helped him to do so. They made the captain a present of 25 guineas, along with thanks for saving property worth at least £22,000.

A SURGEON ONCE had to cancel a heart operation at Cardiff's University of Wales after taking an hour to find a parking space. The surgeon said he was so stressed by the experience that he was in no condition to operate.

THE GRACEFUL OLD bridge at Pontypridd is famous because of the story behind it. It was built by the Reverend William Edwards and was completed in 1756. At the time it was the largest single-arched bridge in the world. It took Edwards four attempts to finish the bridge successfully. The first bridge was a three-arch stone bridge built in 1746. It was destroyed two years later when a heavy storm caused the

River Taff to flood and the weight and force of debris destroyed the bridge and washed it away. The second bridge was a radical 140-foot single arch span over the river which was intended to prevent the bridge from being destroyed in another flood. Ironically the bridge was nearly finished when a flood washed away the centre timber work and the unfinished structure collapsed.

It was rebuilt and stood for about six weeks before it collapsed again because the structure was not balanced and the keystone was forced out. The Reverend Edwards solved this problem in an ingenious way. The design for his fourth attempt included the addition of three holes in the stonework at each end of the bridge to lighten the structure. It worked and the bridge is in use as a footbridge to this day.

Unfortunately, the bridge was a failure at first since it was only 11 feet wide and so steep that horses had difficulty hauling anything over it. As an enterprise, it was also a failure for the ingenious clergyman and left him in debt. He had been paid £500 to build a bridge but it actually cost him nearly £1,200. It is said that local gentry took pity on Edwards and raised a generous subscription to pay off his debts. The Reverend Edwards was undaunted by his setbacks and continued building bridges all over Wales. His three sons also caught the bug and all were involved in bridge-building.

In July 2007 Dave Barclay flew 4,000 miles home to Cardiff from Canada to attend his friend's wedding, only to discover that he was a year too early. Barclay, who was working as a teacher in Toronto, paid £500 for his ticket home after his friend Dave Best had informed him by email earlier in the year that he was getting married on 6 July. It was only when he arrived home and rang Best to find out where the wedding was that he learned that the wedding date was actually 6 July 2008. Barclay later told a journalist, 'At least it's assured me of a mention in the speech next year.'

FOR A SMALL wager a Swansea man undertook to carry out an odd feat in a field near the town on 22 October 1805. He bet that he could pick up one hundred stones arranged at a distance of a yard from each other, one at a time and put them in a basket at the starting point. He had thirty-nine minutes to perform this task and he lost the bet by only a few seconds.

On 19 April 1841 Thomas Price from Llanarth, Cardiganshire, undertook an identical wager. He had an hour to complete the task, but managed to do it in forty-five minutes. The distance both men had to cover to perform the feat was nearly six miles.

JOHN JONES OR Siôn y Gof (John the blacksmith) from Ystumtuen, Cardiganshire, worked in the lead mines at Dylife. He murdered his wife and two children and threw their bodies down an old mineshaft. When the corpses were discovered a short while later, Jones was put on trial and found guilty of the murders. He was hanged on nearby Gallows Hill in October 1719 and his body was put in a gibbet as a warning to other malefactors. In July 1938 two men digging on Gallows Hill unearthed part of the gibbet frame and Jones's skull. These may be seen on display at the St Fagan's National History Museum, Cardiff.

IN SEPTEMBER 2007 motorists using a town centre car park in Llanfyllin, Montgomeryshire, faced the prospect of having to pay to use part of it because one of the owners wished to introduce a charge for parking. Powys County Council owned half of the cark park and Llanfyllin Town Council owned the other half. While Powys wished to introduce paid car parking, Llanfyllin was as determined to keep its side free.

JOHN GRIFFITH OF Holt, Denbighshire, died in 1805 aged 103 years. He was a remarkable man. At the age of ninety he found some geese trespassing in his meadow. Griffith immediately stripped himself naked, drove the geese into the river and, like another goose, swam after them to Holt Bridge, a quarter of a mile away. There he drove them on shore and, still in a state of complete nudity, followed them up to the town 'with utmost sangfroid' to the penfold. Having seen the 'winged depredators' safely penned, Griffith calmly walked home.

HARRY BASKERVILLE AND his fellow workmen were moving a telegraph pole and fastening a wire to a chimney near the bridge shop in Llandysul, Cardiganshire, on 27 May 1895 when the wire snapped, pulling him off the ladder and swinging him clean over the rooftop. As he fell to the ground, Baskerville had just enough time to shout a warning to a man who was directly below him. The man quickly moved out of the way, thereby escaping serious injury. Baskerville was not so lucky. He hit the ground with his side and hand and fractured his forearm. His ankle was also slightly injured. Fortunately, a medical student happened to be on the spot and examined Baskerville; he then took him to have the arm set. Afterwards the bruised and injured man headed home to Carmarthen, well aware of how lucky he was to escape such a bad fall with only minor injuries.

IN SEPTEMBER 1805 a young man was tarred and feathered near Merthyr Tydfil, Glamorgan, for jilting a young woman at the altar. This was the third woman he had left standing on her wedding day.

SWALLOWS BUILT A nest in a lampshade in a bedroom of a home in Rhyl in 1954. The owner of the house, a Mr Rees, was awoken one morning by a pair of swallows building a nest in the lampshade hanging over his bed. Rees gave up his bedroom until the birds had hatched four eggs and reared their offspring.

A DOG MADE a 130-mile journey clinging to a lorry's petrol tank on 17 November 1981. It was found terrified and covered with oil at Bridgend Timber Produce, Bridgend, Glamorgan. The lorry had travelled from Shoreham in Sussex and had made one stop at Leigh Delamare Services, near Swindon. After he was calmed and cleaned up a bit, the dog settled down. Staff gave him a wash and a good meal. 'Lucky', as he was christened, was obviously well-cared for and was very friendly. It was a miracle that he was still alive after such a journey. An appeal was made for the owner of the dog, which was described as part sheepdog, mainly grey, with a black face.

IN JULY 1804 two men were whipped at the cart's tail through Monmouth after being found guilty of numerous petty thefts in the town. Such was the daring impudence of the man who had been the first to receive his punishment that, as soon as he was released, he put on his clothes and calmly followed the cart to witness the flogging of his companion.

IT WAS A case of whisky galore for the inhabitants of Kenfig, Glamorgan, in April 1808, when the *Perseverance* was wrecked on the nearby coastline. Fortunately, the crew were saved. The ship's cargo included files of whisky and the inhabitants eagerly 'saved' this too. They proceeded to drink themselves into a stupor on the unexpected bounty. Two people died from overindulgence and a great many more became very ill.

AT THE AGE of 109, Mrs Watkins of Glamorgan made a trip from Wales to London in 1789 to see the famous actress Sarah Siddons on stage. She made nine visits to the theatre during her stay. Besides this, she sat for her portrait and climbed to the Whispering Gallery in St Paul's Cathedral. Mrs Watkins got home safely after an enjoyable adventure to the capital. She died the following year. For the last thirty years of her life this remarkable woman lived mostly on potatoes.

In June 1806 a row at St Bride's Major, Glamorgan, ended 'in a brutal mode of Welsh fighting, wherein a man received a blow on the side of the head from a stone, and died soon after.' At the subsequent trial the jury's verdict was 'Died by the visitation of God!'

Two grandmothers were banned for life from a Bridgend bingo hall in December 2002 after fighting over a lucky chair. Security staff had to separate the women as 500 other players looked on in amazement. The women were banned after a violent brawl in which one of them suffered a broken nose and two black eyes.

A careless sportsman firing at a cock sparrow in a hedge near the Lower Rope Walk in Swansea, in December 1807, accidentally blasted the hat off a man, who was working on the other side of the hedge. Although the poor man was shaken up he was otherwise unharmed; if the gun had been fired an inch lower, he would have been killed.

The *Cambrian* newspaper of 20 April 1805 commented on a new mode of fashion: 'Several of our young dames of distinction now sport *muslin trowsers* under a white petticoat short enough to exhibit them in full view. It is, however, a moot point at present whether this new fashion be intended to conceal indifferent legs or to draw the gazer's eye more attractively to good ones.'

ALAN WILLIAMS WAS cycling home from work in Wrexham in December 1991 when a badger ran out in front of him. He collided with the animal and was thrown from his bicycle, landing on his face, badly cutting his eye. His expensive £400 hand-assembled bicycle was left beyond repair. The unfortunate cyclist claimed compensation but was told that badgers were the only type of animal not covered by the claim!

AT THE ASSIZES at Monmouth in August 1802, William Sanders, an elderly man from Pontypool, was found guilty of manslaughter, but was discharged after paying a fine of six shillings and eight pence. It was a tragic case. His son had regularly beaten the old man violently with a stick and horsewhip and had threatened to kill him when the first opportunity arose. His father had had enough and 'loaded his gun, and presenting it at the natural reprobate, shot him'.

TWO PRISONERS IN their early twenties broke out of Swansea Magistrates' Court on 6 January 1982 and ran on either side of a lamp-post, forgetting that they were handcuffed together. They broke their wrists. Both later appeared in court on theft charges, with their arms in plaster casts.

WHILE WALKING THROUGH a wood in the Piercefield estate near Chepstow in Monmouthshire on 8 November 1802, a man got tangled up in a net that poachers had spread out to catch game. While he was trying to free himself, three men emerged from hiding behind a nearby hedge and attacked him ferociously. Then they dragged him to a nearby precipice projecting over a river and threw him over.

Fortunately, the victim fell into a part of the river that was just deep enough to cushion his fall, but shallow enough to allow him to stand up. He was unable to free himself from the net and remained partially immersed in the river for the rest of the night and part of the next day before he was discovered. The helpless man was rescued and taken to nearby Piercefield House, where the owner immediately sent for a doctor. Despite his ordeal, his injuries were relatively minor. One leg was dislocated and he was badly bruised and freezing from his immersion in the river, but the poor man made a full recovery. His vicious assailants were never found.

IN MARCH 1894 a groom employed by a gentleman from Dyserth, Denbighshire, was kicked to death by a mare belonging to his employer. This gentleman, of course, got rid of the 'brute'. He also gave the groom's job to the dead man's son. One of the son's responsibilities was the care of a foal belonging to the mare that had killed his father. A year later the son himself was kicked by the foal and died.

IN APRIL 1809 William Davies of the Monmouthshire Western Local Militia became unwell. He sought medical treatment at Pontypool, but it gave no relief. He was afterwards advised to drink some mineral water from a certain spring in the locality. No sooner had he done so, than Davies vomited up a lizard, which was about 7 inches long from head to tail and had 'two rows of teeth, six up and six down'. Davies said he had been 'subject to very sudden startings from the gnawing of the creature, but he was fast recovering'.

STAFF OF THE Cardiff Infirmary were 'much surprised' on 25 November 1903 to find that a dog had hopped in with a broken leg. With commendable speed the animal was taken to the accident ward and its injury carefully treated, after which the injured animal was fed and looked after until its owner was found.

AN ANGRY CIRCUS elephant picked up a horse and cart at Llanelly in April 1897 and flung them about. Local man Mr Jones of Cefn Farm was driving the cart containing several milk churns, when he accidentally ran over the elephant's foot with one of his cart's wheels while passing it on the road. The animal, 'sperting with rage', picked up the cart with its trunk and threw the horse, cart, and driver with great force into the hedge.

The unfortunate farmer was badly cut on the head. The cart was greatly damaged, and the milk churns were ruined. Fortunately, the horse was not injured. The elephant, which belonged to Lord John Sanger's Circus, had previously rampaged at Glyn Neath, chasing a policeman, savagely attacking a pub and smashing the windows of a house.

IAN WILLIAMS WAS the toast of his team-mates in October 2008 when he scored the winning goal with a fractured foot in a soccer match. Williams had injured his right foot some weeks beforehand and a trip to the hospital revealed that he had fractured it. His foot was put in a cast and he was told that he would not be able to play football for at least eight weeks. A few weeks later Williams's team, Pontlliw FC, were playing Pontarddulais Town, while he remained on the substitutes' bench.

By the eighty-fifth minute the teams were still level and Williams begged his coach to let him on. To his delight, he was allowed to play. Williams threw down his crutches and took off his cast before going onto the pitch. As luck would have it, a chance to score came almost immediately and Williams kicked the ball into the net with his broken foot. 'I could not believe it', said Williams. 'It hurt really bad the minute I struck it. I threw up pretty much straight away and had to be substituted a few minutes later. It was good to score the winning goal, but next time I think I'll wait until my foot's properly healed.'

IN SEPTEMBER 1927 a young Welshwoman, who had been in Australia for only a few weeks, caused a stir when she rode up the steps of a hotel at Windsor, New South Wales, and into the public bar, on horseback. To the astonishment of the barkeeper, she ordered a beer, which she drank while remaining in the saddle, and then rode out again.

A BOAT CONTAINING two men was swamped on 6 July 1883 off Milford Haven, Pembrokeshire. One of the men, named Davies, was saved by his dog, but the other, named Taylor, was drowned. The dog first caught hold of Taylor, but finding that he was not its master, let him go, and swam to Davies, whom it supported until he was picked up by a passing steamer.

ENOCH BELTON WAS crossing the Minera Hills, near Wrexham, on 10 January 1879 when his dog left him and suddenly plunged into a snowdrift. Belton followed, and saw the head of a young girl visible above the snow. With great difficulty he dug her out, but found that she was unconscious. He recognized the girl as 10-year-old Ellen Roberts. She had been visiting her home, and was returning to her work as a servant in Pentre Bias when she became lost in deep snowdrifts. Belton carried her to the safety of the nearest house and a doctor was sent for. The doctor revived the half-frozen girl and treated her. She had been in the snow for some twenty-six hours.

THE SWANSEA STEAMSHIP *Collier*, commanded by Captain Jackson, was proceeding past Penarth Roads in June 1882 when distress cries were heard. The captain turned the ship around to make a search. He found a man in the water, sitting on a ladder and hatch with a bundle of clothes tied fast to it. He was exhausted, but once restoratives had been given, he revived and told the captain his story. His name was Patrick Breene, and he was a sailor from the *Baron Colonsay*, bound from Cardiff to Calcutta. Breene claimed to have been ill-treated and half-starved on this vessel, so he decided to escape, and jumped overboard in the night in order to swim to shore. Captain Jackson dropped Breene off in Swansea and he quickly signed up for a voyage on another vessel.

A BIZARRE CASE of mistaken identity occurred at Templeton, Pembrokeshire, on 17 November 1873. A young sailor, named Thomas Davies, from nearby Narberth, went to visit his uncle at the village. In the afternoon he went to the Poyers Arms for a drink. No sooner had he sat down than the landlady began embracing him as her son. The sailor played along and reciprocated the embrace.

The best things in the house were immediately set before him and Davies was fed and given liquor. Davies drank and ate all given to him. When he got drunk, his 'kind mother' led him to a bedroom to sleep. Hardly had the 'prodigal son' laid his head down to rest than the landlady's husband returned home. He immediately saw that Davies was not his son and had him detained for impersonation, despite his wife's pleas of protests that he *was* their missing son.

The parish constable was called and the long-lost 'son' was bound, not in handcuffs, but in cheesecloths, and conveyed to Narberth. The following day, Davies, now sober and repentant, was brought before the magistrate. Fortunately for him, the magistrate was amused by the case and immediately set the young rogue free.

THE TRANSLATION OF public signage into Welsh has not been without its blunders. When Swansea Council wanted to erect a sign barring heavy goods from a residential road, it looked in-house to get the correct translation of 'No entry for heavy goods vehicles. Residential site only'. Unfortunately, the council contacted the translator by email at a time when he was not available. The council received a reply in Welsh saying 'I am not in the office at the moment. Please send any work to be translated.' The council thought *this* text was the translation and used it on the sign!

In 2006, cyclists travelling between Cardiff and Penarth were met with the bilingual sign telling them 'Cyclists dismount' in English and 'Bladder inflammation upset' in Welsh! In the same year a sign for Cardiff pedestrians read 'Look Right' in English and 'Look Left' in Welsh.

In May 1986 a police helmet was lost when a constable was climbing from a ship off Colwyn Bay, Denbighshire. The following month the helmet was found on the shores of the Isle of Man, seventy miles away.

Guests at the Castle Hotel in Neath were enjoying an evening drink in August 2009 when a live 16-inch dogfish fell from the sky and landed on a canopy above their heads. 'Something hit the canvas of the shelter really hard', said assistant manager Andrea Lewis. 'All the customers jumped up and they could see it moving around. In the end, the porter had to get it off with a brush and put it out of its misery. It was suggested we could have cooked it and served it to guests, but we didn't know where it had been.' Where the fish came from remains a mystery.

It was suggested that the fish was thrown on to the canopy, but there were no cars going by at the time and no bedrooms in the hotel were in use above. It was decided that the fish must have been dropped by a passing bird. 'An osprey is really the only bird which could catch and carry a fish like that', said a Royal Society for the Protection of Birds spokeswoman. She said it could 'very well be' one of two ospreys that recently left the nest of the only breeding pair in Wales.

VISITORS TO A church jumble sale in the Memorial Hall Church at New Quay, Cardiganshire, before Easter 2003, picked up bargains when valuable church antiques worth around £10,000 were sold by mistake at the jumble sale for just a few pounds. The precious items included a gold chalice, a silver goblet and ornate candlesticks. The church valuables had been stored in the same room as items for the jumble sale and the mistake occurred when the items got mixed up. When news of the blunder emerged, many of those who had bought the items returned them. By May most of the objects had been returned, but there were still some valuables missing.

IN SEPTEMBER 1807 a chicken killed in Swansea was found to have two hearts.

A RETIRED PRISON officer and his wife became an historic jail's first inmates in a hundred years when staff at the tourist attraction accidentally locked them in. Norman

Bradshaw and his wife June were still looking around Ruthin Jail in Denbighshire in July 2009 when staff locked up for the night, unaware they were still inside. They were trapped in the souvenir shop, but shouted for help and were heard by people working at a building next door. They were freed an hour later when someone with a key was tracked down. The couple received an apology and a refund from Denbighshire Council. Mr Bradshaw had worked as a prison officer for nearly forty years and said, 'During all that time I was never locked inside a prison with no escape – that is until now.'

A NOVEL EXPERIMENT was made on 17 April 1807 on the Swansea to Mumbles railway, which had opened the previous month. The experiment was to gauge the viability of using wind rather than horses to power a carriage along the track. Some sailors rigged a sail on a waggon and, with a strong wind blowing, the 'land ship' set off. They covered the distance of 4½ miles in about three-quarters of an hour. This was a remarkable achievement by a vehicle solely propelled by a sail.

IN NOVEMBER 2002 a gang of thieves smashed their way into a Swansea warehouse and escaped with a huge haul of televisions, video recorders and DVD players. They believed that they had netted themselves a small fortune, but actually all the items were broken. They had been stored in the warehouse on their way back to the manufacturer after shops had returned them for various faults.

In July 1941 10-year-old Margaret Coushin of High Street, Cardigan, was swimming on the Cardigan side of the River Teifi estuary when she was carried away by the current and swept about a mile towards Poppit Sands on the Pembrokeshire side. Southern Dexter from St Dogmaels was fishing when he noticed a man on the opposite shore waving. At first Dexter saw no reason for the man's alarm, then a few moments later he saw something floating upstream. He cast at the object and hooked it. When he drew it ashore, he found it was a child and that he had hooked her bathing costume. She was alive and begged him to save her. She was terribly cold but otherwise all right. Dexter ran with the child in his arms to a nearby house where the owners gave Margaret hot tea and put her to bed.

The bowler hat of a pedestrian was hit by the drive of a golfer at Rhymney and Tredegar Golf Club, Monmouthshire, on 10 September 1934. The man fell, but his head was only slightly grazed. The ball had gone through the hat.

Wood's British Gazetteer of 24 April 1773 records an odd race that had taken place seven days earlier over a distance of a mile on the road between Redbourn and St Albans in Hertfordshire. It was between a labourer and a Welsh girl wearing cumbersome pattens and the girl won the match. Pattens were protective overshoes worn over thin-soled shoes of the era. They were worn by women outdoors in muddy conditions. They resembled clogs and had either wooden soles or thick leather ones.

AMONG THE STRANGEST wills ever admitted to probate was one made by a Welsh hermit, who wrote his will in red chalk on the door of his hut. It was accepted for probate and the door was preserved.

A BIZARRE ACCIDENT occurred at Bala Golf Course, Merionethshire, on 30 September 1929. When the Reverend Davies Jones hit a ball that had landed at the mouth of a rabbit hole, a rabbit suddenly appeared and was killed by the downward motion of the club.

A CARELESS MISTAKE on the part of William Price of Bedwas nearly cost him and his family's lives in March 1889. Price worked at a quarry at Pwllypant, near Caerphilly. He always brought his own tea leaves to work in an old tin. One evening, he mistakenly took home a similar tin, which was half-full of blasting powder. At home Price went to warm up his tea leaves by placing the tin on the house fire. He then sat down near it, cradling his youngest child in his arms. A few minutes later the powder exploded, wrecking the house, breaking windows and destroying furniture. The blast caused considerable damage to a neighbouring cottage. Luckily, Price and his family escaped without a scratch. Considering the force of the explosion, this was little short of a miracle.

MAUREEN PORTER FELL and broke her hip in the garden of her remote cottage near Cenarth, Carmarthenshire, on 24 May 2005. The 69-year-old was too badly injured to move and no neighbours were near enough to hear her cries for help. Night fell and she was in danger of exposure, but Pedro, her 15-year-old border collie, lay close up beside Maureen to keep her warm. He even gently prodded her with his paw throughout the eighteen-hour ordeal, which enabled her to stay conscious.

The next morning she was found, shivering from cold and hoarse from shouting, by local shopkeeper Pat Milner, alerted by Maureen's husband in London, who was worried when she failed to answer the phone. Her husband lavished praise on Pedro: 'It was very dark and cold throughout the night and she could hear owls and foxes. But Pedro made sure she was safe and warm. He is a brilliant dog – and very loyal. We got him from a rescue centre ten years ago and he follows Maureen everywhere. It would have been a different story if Pedro hadn't been there – he saved her life.'

IN 2004, WHILE still in her mother's womb, McKenzie Gwynne of Ebbw Vale, Monmouthshire, had eight transfusions to save her life. Her mother, Catherine, had a condition that was life-threatening to an infant, and the only way to keep McKenzie alive was to give her regular transfusions through the umbilical cord. During one treatment, McKenzie's heart stopped, but she survived thanks to her doctors' care. She was born ten weeks early, weighing 3 lb 7 oz.

COUNCIL WORKERS IN Cardiff were roundly criticized for building an 8-foot long bicycle lane in 2010, at an estimated cost of £2,000. The city's cyclists were puzzled by the logic behind its creation when an official said it was to 'highlight the interface between the eastbound carriageway and the beginning of a new contraflow facility'. To clear up this muddle, a council spokesman added that its purpose was to alert cyclists to a left-hand turn into a new facility.

THREE CHILDREN PLAYING on the beach at Newton Point, Porthcawl, Glamorganshire, were suddenly swept out to sea by a huge wave on 2 August 1992. Moments later, an equally large wave washed them ashore again.

MARK COLLING FROM Llanelli sailed into *The Guinness Book of Records* in 2007 after building a 1:100 scale replica of the *Titanic* using 3.5 million matchsticks. Colling spent almost 17 months constructing the 19-foot model, which weighed almost a ton. He even included the iceberg that sank the vessel on its ill-fated maiden voyage in April 1912.

A MAN LITERALLY escaped by a hair's-breadth on 13 May 1869 after a train passed over him while he lay asleep on the track. The incident happened on the track between Bala and Dolgellau. About a mile and a half from Dolgellau the train was speeding down an incline when the driver suddenly caught sight of a man, apparently fast asleep, lying with his head on the iron rails. The driver frantically blew the whistle to warn the man and tried to slow down the train to give him time to roll away. None of the driver's efforts made any difference.

The sleeping man did not stir and it looked certain

that a shocking fatality would occur. By a stroke of luck, the man turned his head slightly just as the engine wheels reached him, and the train passed over him, only severing some hair from his head. Awakened by the noise of the passing train, the man saw the terrible fate he had just escaped and fled down the track. He was followed and caught by an inspector, who jumped off the train as it screeched to a halt. The man turned out to be a railway employee and he was promptly fired. Accounts vary as to the reason why he had picked such a dangerous spot for a nap. Some say he was drunk, others that he had worked all night and was dropping from exhaustion. All agree he was a very, very lucky man.

A GIANT VERSION of the *Mona Lisa* went on display at Wrexham's Eagles Meadow shopping centre in 2009. The enormous version of Leonardo da Vinci's masterpiece covered 2,600 square feet (240 square metres) and was more than fifty times larger than the original sixteenth-century work which hangs in The Louvre in Paris. Artist Katy Webster was in charge of the project and it took 245 people 987 hours to create the work, using 23 gallons of paint.

STUART CRANE FROM Carmarthen was impaled by a wooden post in November 2000 when his car slid off a busy dual carriageway at 70 mph. As it crashed into a fence, a 28-inch wooden post pierced the driver's door and impaled Stuart through his right side and out the other side. Doctors later told him it was probably his large stomach that saved him by protecting his vital organs. He said later:

It all happened very quickly. I remember opening my eyes, looking down and seeing this bloody great big fence post sticking through my sides. My shirt had been ripped off and forced into my stomach. The weirdest thing was that I didn't feel any pain at all. I was completely numb, but I managed to get my mobile out of my pocket and the first thing I thought of doing was calling my sister Pat. I told her, 'I've been in an accident and I've got a bit of splinter in me.'

Then Stuart called 999 and explained what had happened. At first rescuers were unable to find his car in the dark and Stuart had to stay on the phone and guide them to the wreck when he saw their flashing lights nearby. There they found the 32-year-old trapped tightly in the wreck. Two surgeons were flown by helicopter to the scene to advise on the rescue. They had to work carefully to free Stuart before he could be moved to hospital. He underwent three hours of surgery to remove the post from his stomach. 'They couldn't just slide it out, so they had to cut my stomach open down the middle and pull it out from the front. The post had done a lot of damage internally, but, thankfully, I hadn't lost too much blood.'

Doctors had warned his family that they thought the injuries were too severe and Stuart might die from infection. His injuries were enormous: he had lost two ribs on each side, had a collapsed lung, torn bowels and a ruptured stomach. Stuart's heart stopped four times while doctors worked to save him. Four months and 900 stitches later, he was allowed home. Stuart retained the stake as a souvenir and swore to keep his 21-stone figure and never go on a diet.

Baby Liam Evans from Colwyn Bay, Denbighshire, survived for three days by eating soil in August 1998 after his grandfather's car had crashed down a mountainside. The car had plunged 150 yards and somersaulted before coming to rest at the bottom of a steep slope. 61-year-old retired policeman Gwilym Evans was killed, but his 13-month-old grandson was unharmed. The small child managed to release his seatbelt and crawl through a broken window after the crash and survived by getting moisture from the soil he ate. An inquest heard that thick bracken in the area kept Liam sheltered from too much sunlight in the daytime and from the cold at night. He was rescued close to the Horseshoe Pass, near Llangollen, after 10-year-old Matthew Williams spotted the car wreck when he had wandered off during a family picnic.

Former soldier Philip Loveday from Bridgend has lived with a broken neck since 1970. It was only properly diagnosed in 2012 when he was sent for an MRI scan after dislocating his shoulder. In the meantime he had an active career in the army, continued playing rugby, practising martial arts and enjoying pursuits such as mountain-biking and paragliding.

Aged just sixteen, Philip had broken his neck in 1970 while playing rugby. It was diagnosed as a fracture and treated. He broke it again in 1971. When he was passed fit in a medical examination, he thought that the fracture had healed. At the time the army told him to bulk up if he wanted to remain in the army, so Loveday transformed from a seven-stone weakling with a tiny neck into a large man with a 22-inch neck. Now Loveday believes that his strong neck muscles have literally kept his head on his shoulders.

DRWYS-Y-COED CHAPEL STOOD at the foot of Clogwyn-y-Barcud, Caernarvonshire. At 5.30 p.m. on 17 February 1892 a huge boulder fell from the side of the mountain and crashed through the roof, leaving no stone standing. Attached to the chapel was a small house, where a local man was laid at rest, attended by a handful of people. There was to have been a prayer meeting that night at 6 p.m. It was usually held at the house where the body was laid out, but that evening it was to have taken place at the chapel. When the giant boulder hit the chapel, the frightened people ran out of the house. Had the boulder fallen a few feet to one side, it would have killed everyone in the house. Had it come thirty minutes later, when the meeting was on, not a person there would have survived. The damage to the chapel was so extensive, it was beyond repair. In time, the resilient local residents built a new chapel on a safer site across the road from the ruins of the old one. The boulder still remains where it landed.

TONY EVANS FROM Portmead, Swansea, spent five years knotting together 6 million elastic bands to create a giant rubber ball that weighed 2,600 lb. The huge rubber ball had a circumference of 14 feet 8 inches. In 2003 the producers of the *Ripley's Believe it or Not* television series offered Tony the chance to see what would happen when the rubber-band ball was dropped from a plane. Would it bounce or would it explode? The ball was shipped across the Atlantic and brought on a tour of the United States, before being loaded on a plane.

At a specific location in the Mojave Desert, the rubber ball was dropped from the plane a mile from the ground. For safety reasons the producers had cleared a space of one square mile around the drop zone. It took twenty seconds for the rubber ball to hit the ground. 'There was a huge cloud of dust which went about 15–20 feet into the air,' Evans reported, 'but we didn't see the ball bounce back up.' When they raced to the scene, they found a huge 9-foot wide crater, with the ball a few feet away from it. Thousands of elastic bands were everywhere as the impact had roughed up the ball considerably.

POSTMAN GERALD LLOYD stopped deliveries to the village of Wiseman's Bridge near Tenby in March 1999 because of repeated attacks by a local pheasant known as Henry. Villagers were forced to make a fourteen-mile round trip to pick up their post. Just days before Lloyd was due to try to resume his rounds in the village, Henry was found dead after being hit by a vehicle.

A few years later another Welsh postman was the victim of a second pheasant with a disliking for postal staff. Delano Thomas was frequently attacked by a pheasant known as Fred as he made his deliveries in the village of Moylegrove, Pembrokeshire, in 2004.

TONY LLOYD FROM Cardiff has a collection of over 4,000 refrigerator magnets from around the world.

ON 10 JANUARY 2009, 140 scuba divers ventured to the bottom of a flooded rock quarry in Chepstow to iron clothes simultaneously and set a new record. Each diver had to iron one item of clothing within a ten-minute time limit at the bottom of the 173-foot deep quarry. Eighty-six of the divers managed to complete the task successfully, beating the previous world record of seventy-two set in Melbourne, Australia, the year before, and raised £10,000 for the Royal National Lifeboat Institution.

A FEROCIOUS BULL charged at a train near Llandeilo in Carmarthenshire on 12 June 1881, killing itself and throwing two carriages off the railway line. All the passengers on board were shaken by the experience, but otherwise unharmed. They were transferred to fresh carriages and the train resumed its journey.

LITTLE OLIVE DRING from Swansea endured an uncomfortable experience in July 1906. Her mother had sent the 4-year-old to the pantry to fetch something. Olive frightened a mouse which was on a shelf level with her mouth and it suddenly jumped down her throat. Olive ran back to the kitchen and fell down choking. Her mother stuck her fingers down her daughter's throat as far as possible and felt something soft disappear down it. She immediately administered emetics and Olive subsequently recovered from the strange experience.

A BLIND MAN under study at Bangor University in 2004 astonished scientists by appearing to be able to read the emotions on people's faces. He was capable of identifying angry, sad and happy faces with an accuracy of 59 per cent – significantly higher than would be expected by chance.

MICHAEL HANSON AND Hayley Morgan had a bovine-themed wedding at Llandefalle, near Talgarth, Breconshire, in 2012. Dressed in a pair of white wellington boots, the bride arrived at the church aboard a tractor. After the service, the tractor transported the happy couple to a field on Hayley's parents' farm where they had a wedding portrait taken with a herd of cattle.

KEITH JACKSON WORKS for industrial paint manufacturers Aqua Tec Coatings in Wrexham and is paid to watch paint dry. It is easy to regard his job as an amusing one, but it is a vital one for the company. In his position as technical manager, Jackson is charged with formulating paint that dries as quickly as possible. This type of paint is essential for a great number of businesses, such as the London Underground, whose stations are not closed to passengers for more than a couple of hours a night. Once a station's walls and floors are painted, they have to dry speedily enough for passengers to use the station when it reopens early the day. Aqua Tec's paints can dry in as little as thirty minutes, and it is Jackson's job to test them under an array of situations.

THE REGISTER OF St Crallo's Church, Coychurch, near Bridgend, Glamorganshire, records that in 1771 a wedding ceremony was repeated a month later because the bridegroom had placed the ring on the bride's wrong finger.

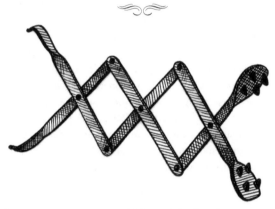

DOG TONGS WERE once widely used in churches to remove disruptive dogs during services. A set of these unusual implements can be seen on display at St Beuno's Church, Clynnog Fawr, Caernarvonshire.

SARAH JACOBS (1857–69) from Carmarthenshire was popularly known as 'The Welsh Fasting Girl'. She attracted great attention because, according to her parents, she had not eaten any food at all since the age of ten. For a long period she enjoyed a great deal of publicity and received numerous gifts from people who believed her condition was miraculous. Doctors were more sceptical and proposed that Sarah be monitored under strict medical attention to prove the validity of her claims. Her parents agreed and Sarah was put under a constant watch by a team of nurses, who were instructed to give her food if she asked for it, but otherwise were to do nothing.

After two weeks, they reported that the girl was showing clear signs of starvation. Her parents refused to heed advice urging that she be fed. A few days later the girl died. Her parents were later convicted of manslaughter and jailed for several months.

There are two similar cases from Wales. Gaenor Hughes from Bodelith, Llandderfel, Merionethshire, was said to have lived on nothing but water from a spring near her home for six years before her death in 1780. Nearly a century later, Ann Morgan from Borth, Cardiganshire, reputedly went without food and drink for several weeks before receiving medical treatment, which probably saved her life.

DR RICHARD GRIFFITHS (1758–1826), a wealthy eccentric from Llanwonno, a hamlet north of Pontypridd, Glamorganshire, once won 500 guineas on a snail race, by an underhand trick. He fooled his opponent, pretending to prick his snail to make it go faster. The other man followed suit and actually pricked his snail, making it curl up and come to a standstill. Griffiths had a mischievous sense of humour. He left eccentric instructions for his funeral, directing that he was to be carried by six specifically named people, who were all lame.

TWO RECORDED CASES of dreams have resulted in positive outcomes. The first is the tale of a man who was saved from death because of a dream. The Reverend Richard

Boardman had been preaching in Mold, Flintshire, one night in the late eighteenth century and was making his way across the Dee estuary to Parkgate in Cheshire, as quickly as he could on horseback, when the tide came in faster than he'd expected. The water rose so fast that the Reverend Boardman could neither proceed nor go back to reach safety. In this perilous position the preacher gave himself up for lost and made his peace.

Then he saw two men run down a hill, get into a boat and come to his aid. They got to him just as the sea reached his knees, as he sat on horseback. Boardman's rescuers pulled him aboard and headed back to shore, towing the swimming horse. One of the clergyman's rescuers told him:

> Last night I dreamed I must get to the top of such a hill. When I awoke, the dream made such an impression on my mind that I could not rest. I went and called my friend, and urged him to accompany me. When we came to the place, we saw nothing more than usual. However, I begged him to go with me to another hill at a small distance, and there we saw your distressed situation.

The Reverend Boardman was very lucky that his rescuer had followed his instincts. The previous month another traveller had been trapped in the same situation and tried to swim for shore with his horse. Both man and animal had been drowned.

IFOR BACH WAS a twelfth-century Welsh lord in Senghenydd, a part of Wales that was not entirely under Norman control.

Annoyed that his Norman overlord, William, Earl of Gloucester, was trying to take land which, under Welsh law, belonged to him, Ifor Bach decided on a daring stratagem to regain his lands. One night in 1158 he scaled the walls of Cardiff Castle, using his bare hands, seized the Earl, his wife and their young son, and conveyed them to his stronghold. It is said that he refused to release them until he had recovered the land he had lost 'and a lot more'.

A STORY RECORDED in *The Proceedings of the Society for Psychical Research* tells that on 3 October 1871 a Miss Phillips of Church Bank, Welshpool, Montgomeryshire, had a deaf and dumb maid who fell ill and needed a change of air. Miss Phillips proposed to send the girl to her brother for a few weeks' rest, but the girl did not want to go and was nowhere to be seen on the morning she was to depart. The house was searched from top to bottom, but the girl had disappeared.

The police were immediately informed but failed to locate the missing girl. Three days later local policeman Inspector Strefford called and asked to be allowed to make a search of the house. Miss Phillips gave him permission and the policeman, who had never been in the house before, went straight to the cellar and found the girl. She was in an open flue directly beneath the fireplace in the room above. The hole through which she had crawled into her hiding place was very small and she was unable to free herself. The brick wall was quickly broken down and the girl was released.

Inspector Strefford revealed that the girl's rescue was the consequence of a dream. He had woken in the middle of the night and told his wife: 'I know where that poor girl is. She is up a chimney in a cellar belonging to the house in which she lives.'

ACCORDING TO *THE Guinness Book of Records* the tallest Welshman on record is William Evans (1599–1634) of Monmouthshire, who was porter to King Charles I. He was 7 feet 6 inches tall.

THE WHISTLING SANDS is a curious beach on the Lleyn Peninsula in Caernarvonshire, near Aberdaron. The smooth white sand actually squeaks or whistles as you walk across it. The sound is made when the unusually shaped grains rub together when compressed.

THE WELSH NATIONAL anthem, '*Hen Wlad Fy Nhadau* ' ('Land of My Fathers') was written in 1856. James James (1833–1902) from Pontypridd composed the song's melody, to which his father Evan James (1809–78) added the lyrics.

BEAUMARIS JAIL IN Anglesey was opened in 1829 and was a shining example of the Victorian penal system. It is now a museum where curious visitors can see the conditions where prisoners were kept and punished. The jail has the only surviving tread wheel in Britain. This was a form of punishment for prisoners sentenced to hard labour. The prisoner was forced to step up repeatedly on a giant wheel to keep it rotating.

THE AMAZING GRAVESTONE of John Renie lies in the graveyard of St Mary's Church in Monmouth. Renie was a complex character. He was a skilled tradesman and active political and social reformer. Unusually, he designed and carved his own curious gravestone. On it his epitaph, 'Here Lies John Renie', is written in the form of an acrostic and can be read in multiple directions. It is said the inscription can be read in over 40,000 different ways. Tragically, Renie died in 1832 at the age of thirty-three.

MARGARET EVANS (1696–*c.* 1801) from Penllyn, near Cowbridge, Glamorganshire, was a remarkable woman. Evans was a keen huntswoman and kept her own pack of hounds. She was also an expert carpenter, blacksmith and shoemaker and a talented musician. Even at the age of seventy Evans was a noted wrestler and few dared to wrestle with her. It is said that her husband agreed to marry her after she beat him up. After a second thrashing, he became a Methodist and later was a devout leader in the area.

RICHARD JOHN LLOYD Price (1843–1923) is buried in a mausoleum with a curious pyramid-shaped roof in the graveyard of Llanfor Church, near Bala, Merionethshire. It is said that he was saved from financial ruin after winning a large wager on Bendigo, the horse that won the Jubilee Stakes at Kempton Park in 1887. With some of the winnings Lloyd Price built the mausoleum and had the following curious epitaph inscribed over the doorway:

As to my latter end I go,
To win my Jubilee,
I bless the good horse Bendigo,
Who built this tomb for me.

IN THE TENTH century King Edgar of England demanded a yearly tribute from the Welsh King Hywel Dda of 300 wolf heads. Hywel kept up the payment for three or four years, after which he complained that there were not enough wolves left to pay the tribute.

WILLIAM DAVIES (1627–90) from Wrexham was a respectable farmer and father of eighteen. He was also a successful highwayman for over forty years. As a young man he married and settled in Bagshot, Surrey, and took to highway robbery to supplement his living. Finally he was captured and executed. His corpse was afterwards strung up in chains on Bagshot Heath as a warning to other would-be malefactors.

JEMIMA NICHOLAS (1750–1832), a cobbler-woman of Fishguard, Pembrokeshire, performed heroic service and became a national heroine on 22 February 1797 when an invasion force of 1,400 French troops landed near Fishguard. Despite their numbers, they were easily subdued by local militia and forced to surrender. When Jemima came across a dozen stragglers on her property she rounded them up with a pitchfork and marched them down to the local lock-up. Because of her actions, she was awarded an annual pension of £50.

BARTHOLOMEW ROBERTS (1682–1722) from Little Newcastle in Pembrokeshire was the most successful pirate of his time. Between 1719 and 1722 he captured over 470 ships, stripping them of their cargoes and valuables.

THE REVEREND NESTOR Williams went fishing at Pentwyn Reservoir, Breconshire, on 5 September 1874 and caught a hare instead of a fish. The animal was swimming in the lake when the clergyman hooked and landed it.

JOHN THOMAS EVANS (1770–99) from Waunfawr, Caernarvonshire, was an unlikely explorer. In his day some believed that Prince Madoc had discovered America in the twelfth century. There was a persistent rumour that the Welsh-speaking descendants of these Welsh explorers still lived in America. Vague reports added credence to the existence in North Dakota of a tribe of fair-skinned or 'Welsh Indians' called the Mandans.

In 1792 Evans decided to head to America to investigate the truth of this for himself. In St Louis in Spanish Louisiana he was arrested and locked up as a British spy. After two years he was released when he agreed to go with an expedition to explore the Missouri and try to find a way through the Rocky Mountains to the Pacific Coast from its headwaters. Evans was happy to go along as it would bring him close to the Mandans. After travelling through largely unknown lands and braving hostile tribes and harsh conditions, Evans finally reached the Mandan settlement.

Disappointingly, it was quickly clear to him that they did not speak Welsh and were not the mythical lost tribe for which he had been searching. All the same, they made him welcome and he stayed with them for several months before heading back to St Louis in 1797.

In a letter, to a friend, Evans concluded: 'having explored and charted the Missouri for 1,000 miles and by my communication with the Indians this side of the Pacific Ocean from 35 to 49 degrees of latitude, I am able to inform you that there no such people as the Welsh Indians.' Two years later he drank himself to death in New Orleans, a broken man.

Despite the failure of his eccentric quest, Evans' hazardous journey was not a complete failure. A map he made of the route he took was used by Lewis and Clark, leaders of the first overland expedition to the Pacific Coast.

CARDIFF-BORN 'CAPTAIN' WILLIAM George Auger (1881–1922) was extremely tall and known as the Cardiff Giant. His parents were of average size, but Auger grew to over 7 feet 6 inches high, although he was billed as standing over 8 feet high. As a young man, he served as a policeman, first in Cardiff, then in London. When Auger and his 5 foot 4 inch wife Bertha attended the Barnum and Bailey circus, they found he was a full head taller than the resident circus giant. He was quickly hired on the spot and spent several years touring with the circus. In 1906 he wrote and starred in a play called *Jack, The Giant Killer*. It was extremely successful and ran for ten years. The Augers made their home in Fairfield, Connecticut, and settled down to a comfortable life. In 1922 the lure of the stage was too great and Auger made another tour. The same year he was approached by silent film star Harold Lloyd about appearing in his film *Why Worry?* Auger was delighted and agreed, but died before the film went into production.

FOR A SMALL wager, a young Beaumaris man undertook to eat sixty raw eggs in twenty minutes in May 1825. He accomplished the feat, then was 'suddenly seized with a sort of spasms, and crowed like a cock for nearly half an hour.'

TREVOR WILLIAMS OF Dan y Bryn, Tonna, near Neath, Glamorganshire, witnessed a shower of dried peas fall in his garden in April 1980. 'They were bouncing off the greenhouse and house roof in their thousands', he said. 'The storm lasted several minutes and I was able to collect several jam-jars full of peas.'

FFESTINOG-BORN DR ROBERT Mills Roberts (1862–1935) was known as a fearless goalkeeper. On one occasion in 1897 he agreed to play for Wales against England – despite both his wrists being in plaster and having splints up to his elbows. England beat Wales 4-0.

DURING THE 1893–4 season Preston North End beat Reading 18–0. The Preston goalkeeper that day was Wrexham-born James Trainer (1863–1915). When it started to rain heavily in the second half, Trainer put on a raincoat, taking it off only on the two occasions when his services were briefly required.

MORE THAN 200 people died at the Winter Quarters mine near Scofield, Utah, on 1 May 1900. Many of the victims were Welsh miners. Some of the lucky survivors were, too. James Naylor was blown more than 200 feet by the explosion but made a soft landing and was unhurt. Evan Williams was blown through a door and also survived. Another Welshman, Roderick Davis escaped the explosion, but re-entered the mine to help with the rescue.

He fell unconscious from the foul air and other rescuers presumed that he was another corpse and placed him in a row of dead bodies in the house being used as a temporary morgue. When his body was being washed Davis came to and left under his own steam.

HENRY WILLIAM PAGET, 1st Marquess of Anglesey, (1768–1854) famously lost his leg at the Battle of Waterloo on 18 June 1815, when he was hit by cannon fire. His destroyed leg had to be amputated. Paget was commander of cavalry at the battle. He was said to have been near the Duke of Wellington when the injury occurred. When his leg was hit, Anglesey turned to Wellington and exclaimed, 'By God, sir, I've lost my leg!', to which Wellington calmly replied 'By God, sir, so you have!'

Afterwards, the marquess used an articulated false leg invented by James Potts, which became known as the Anglesey Leg. One of these artificial legs used by the marquess is on display at Plas Newydd in Anglesey, as is the leg of the hussar trousers worn by the nobleman at Waterloo.

TOMMY THOMAS FROM Pontlottyn, in the Rhymney Valley, had a narrow escape from death on 11 April 1907. A train was running into the town's station when the 5-year-old began racing along the platform by the side of the engine. A man rushed forward to stop him, but before he could reach him, the boy stumbled and pitched head-first off the platform, under the very wheels of the engine. When horrified spectators dared to look again, they saw the child lying crying on the far side of the railway tracks. Miraculously, the driving-rod of the engine had caught Tommy as he fell and flung him clear of the wheels. Except for a few bruises, the child was unhurt.